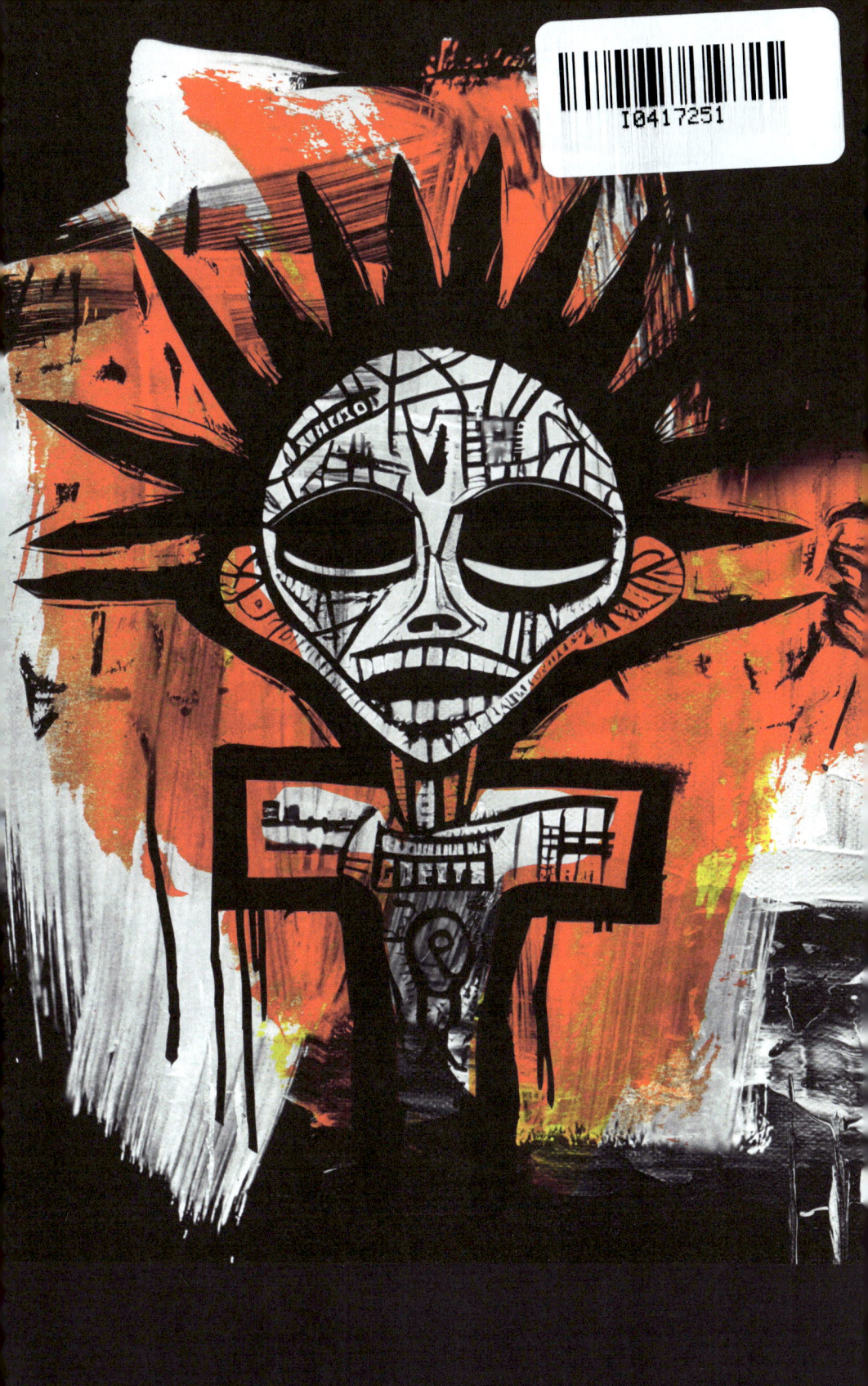

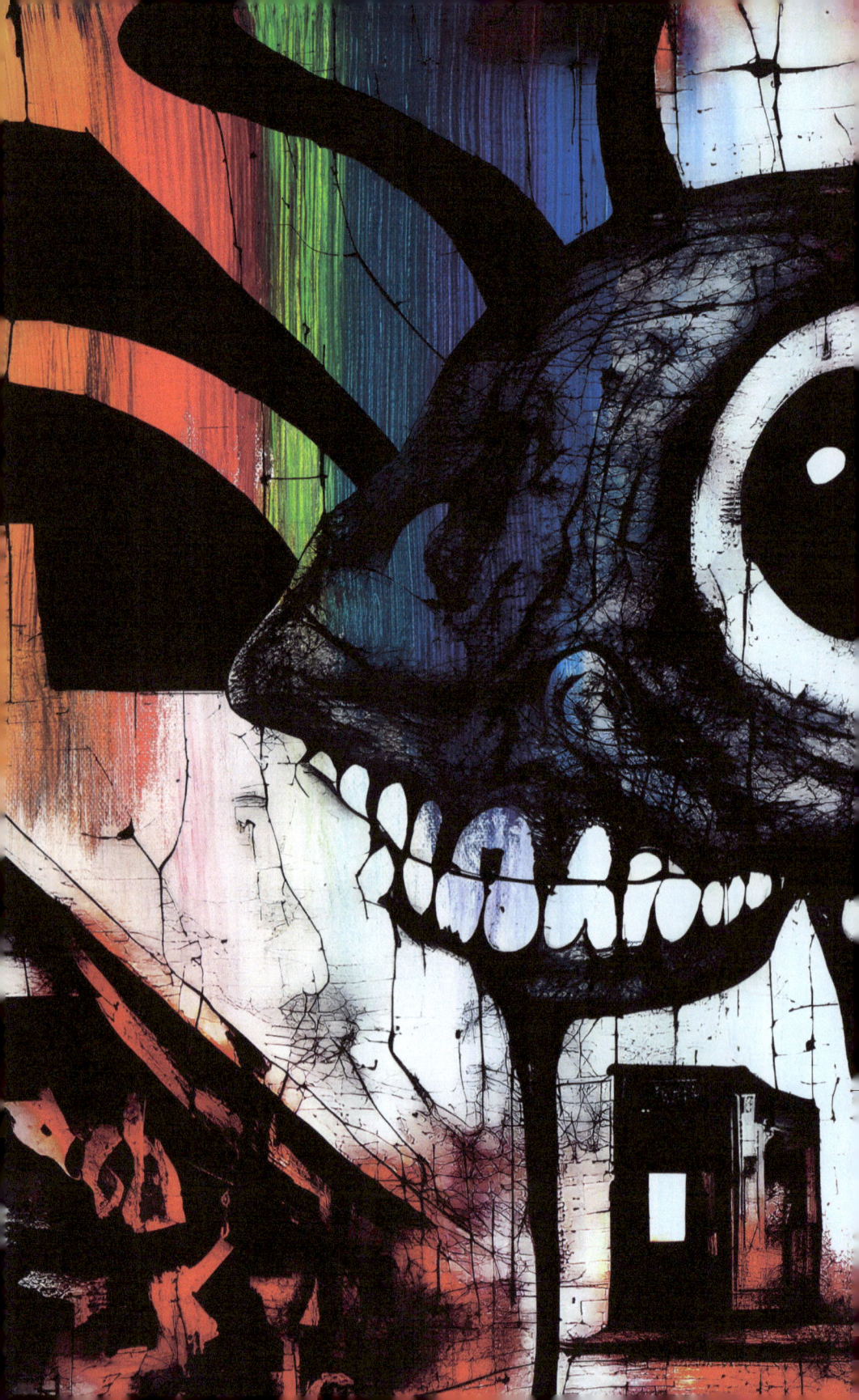

ISSUE NO.

01

Jim Marcus

ARTIST SPOTLIGHT MAGAZINE

TYPOGRAPHER | ILLUSTRATOR | PAINTER | MUSICIAN | WRITER | CULTURE HACKER

This is the first issue of a magazine meant to highlight the art and design work of various artists that are working on the edge today, through music, type, painting, illustration, and more.

Pulseblack has no ownership of the work shown and functions as a publicity outlet for the artists.

November, 2024
ISBN 979-8-9917282-7-0
www.pulseblack.com

Contents

Overview

Jim Marcus

The goal here was to put together a portfoio of work I really enjoyed that has just been done in the last couple of years. That seems easy enough. I've worked with people I really liked a lot on projects I thought were great.

But I kept falling back on the idea that none of it felt coherent. Sure, it felt like a portfolio but it didn't feel like a book - like a magazine. There were corporate things and pretty things and flowy magical things. And those are great, but I felt like it needed a through line

Yes, I know that wasn't the point. But I wanted this to work as a magazine.

So I landed on the idea that I have, at the end of the day, a number of portfolios. But I never really put together a portfolio that acted as a design approach for the dark scene-the industrial and dark music scene that I've been a part of for so long. I realized that I do love.

Even then, there were so many things. So I just abridged this a bit, included some of my own artwork, and had fun.

Again, probably not the point.

But it worked for me.

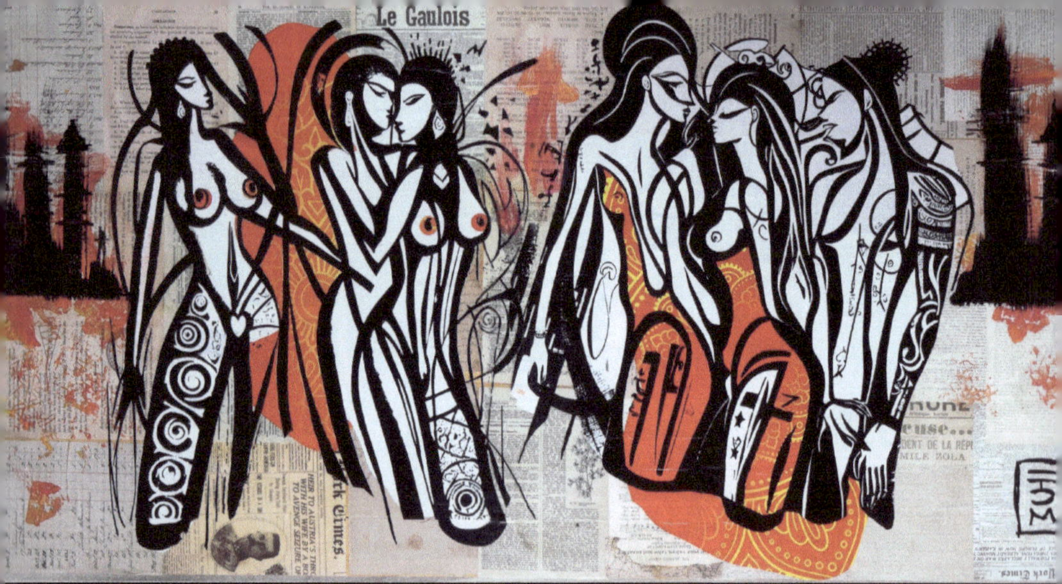

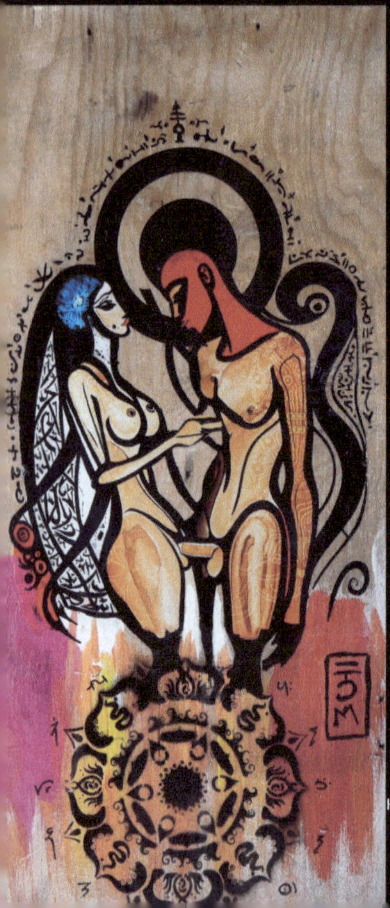

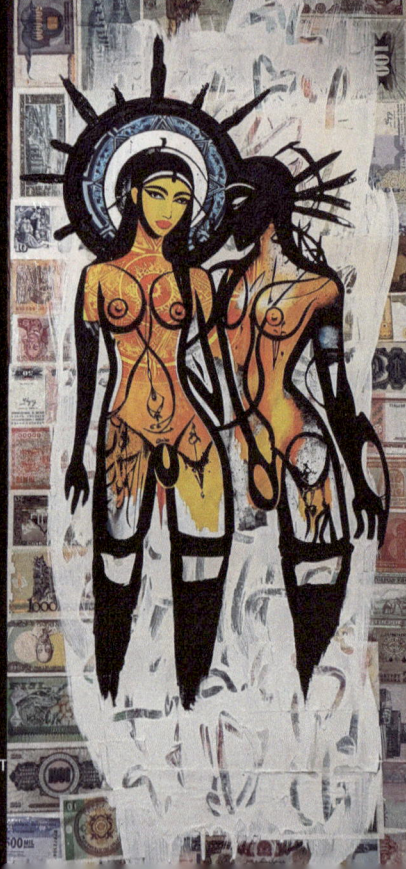
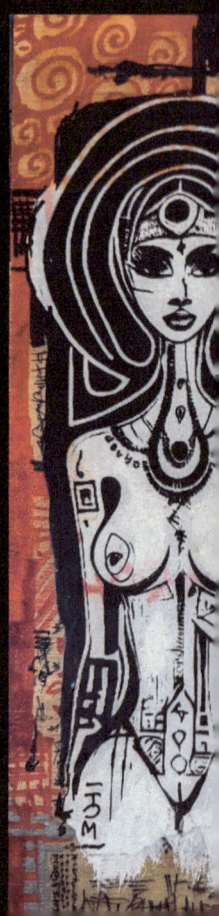

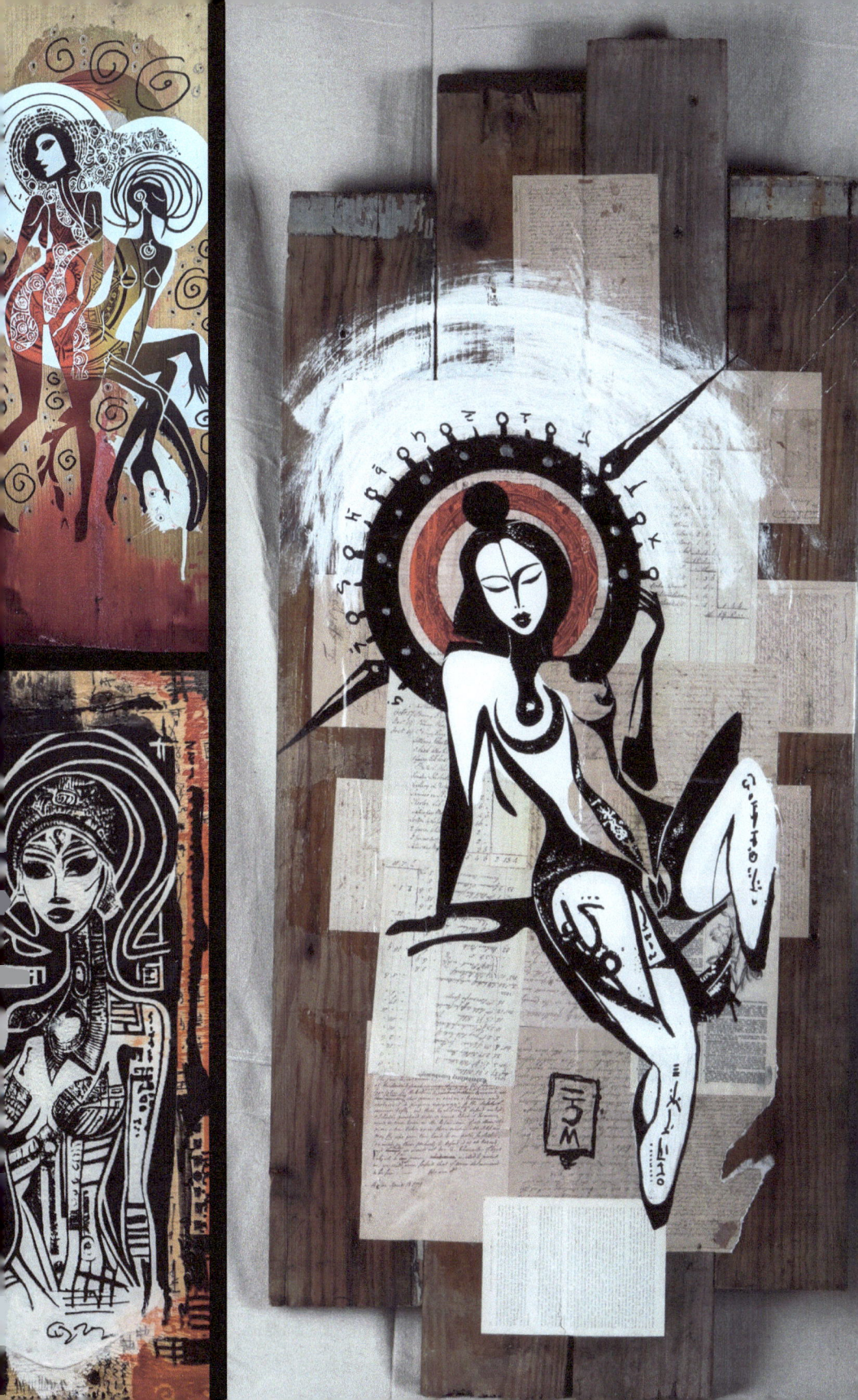

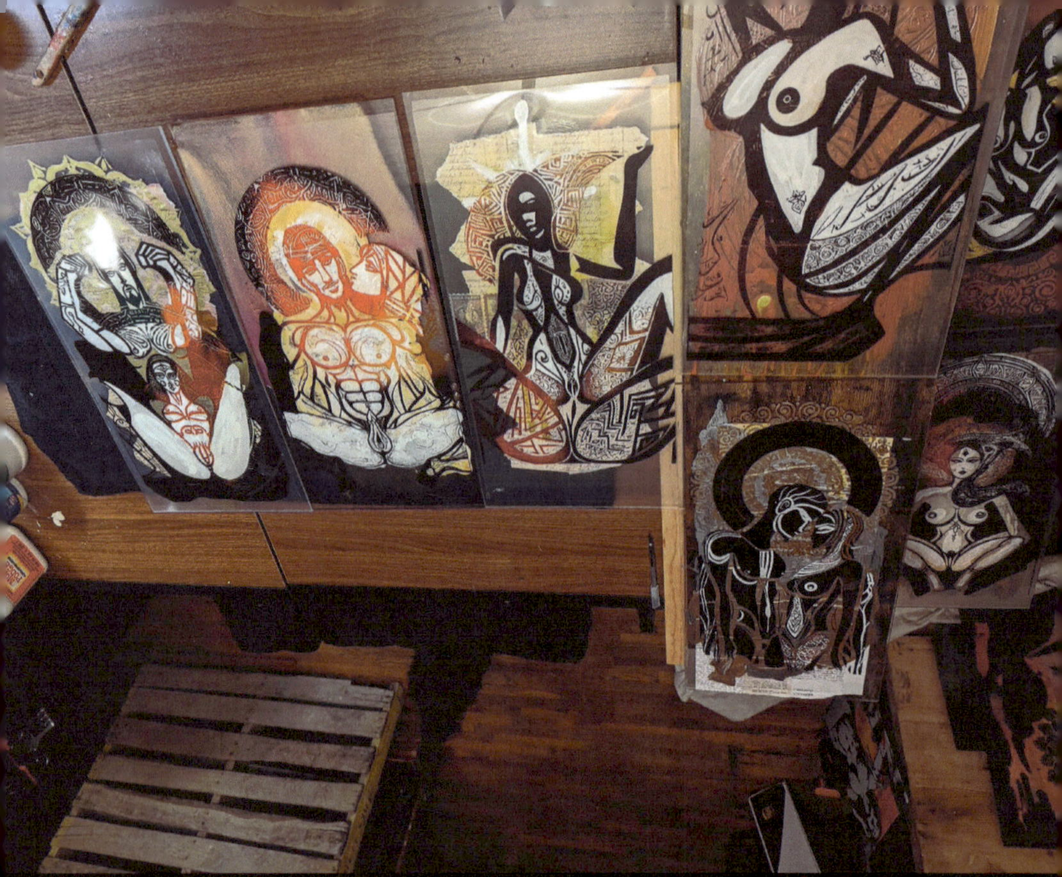

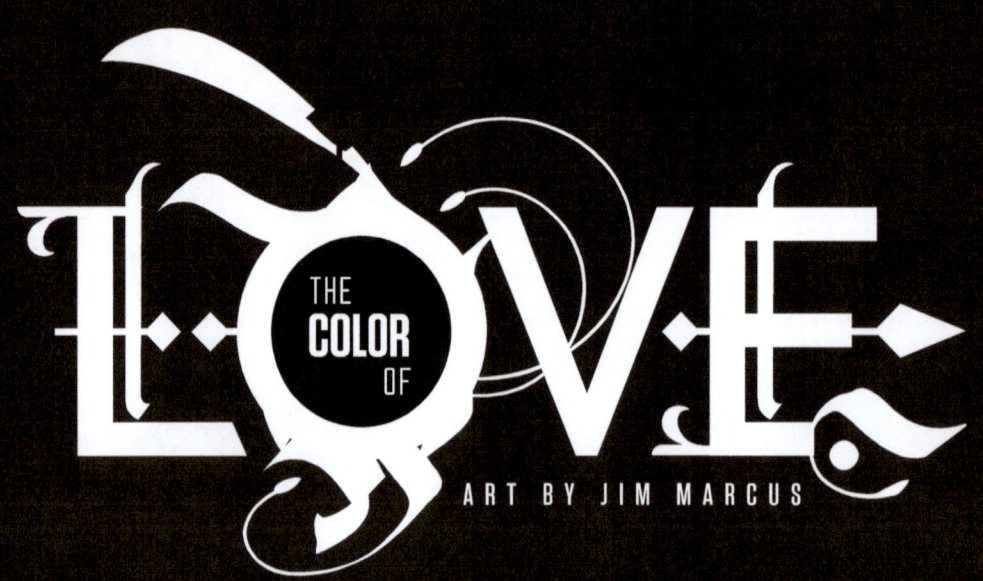

THE COLOR OF LOVE

ART BY JIM MARCUS

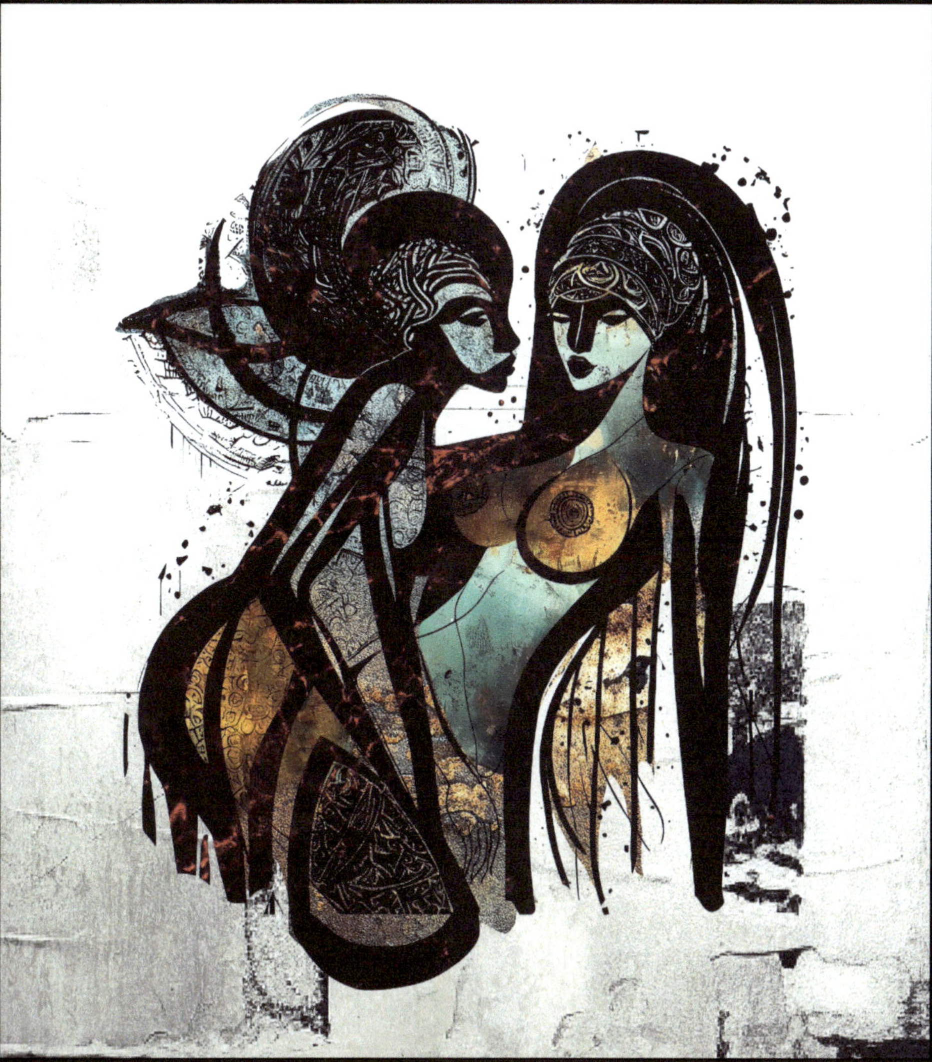

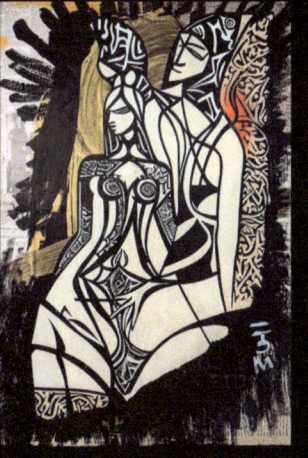
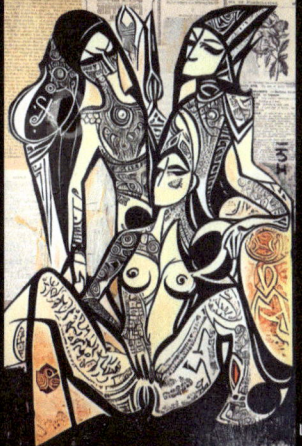
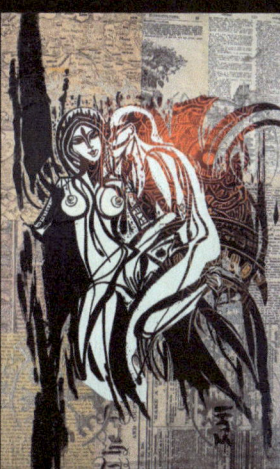

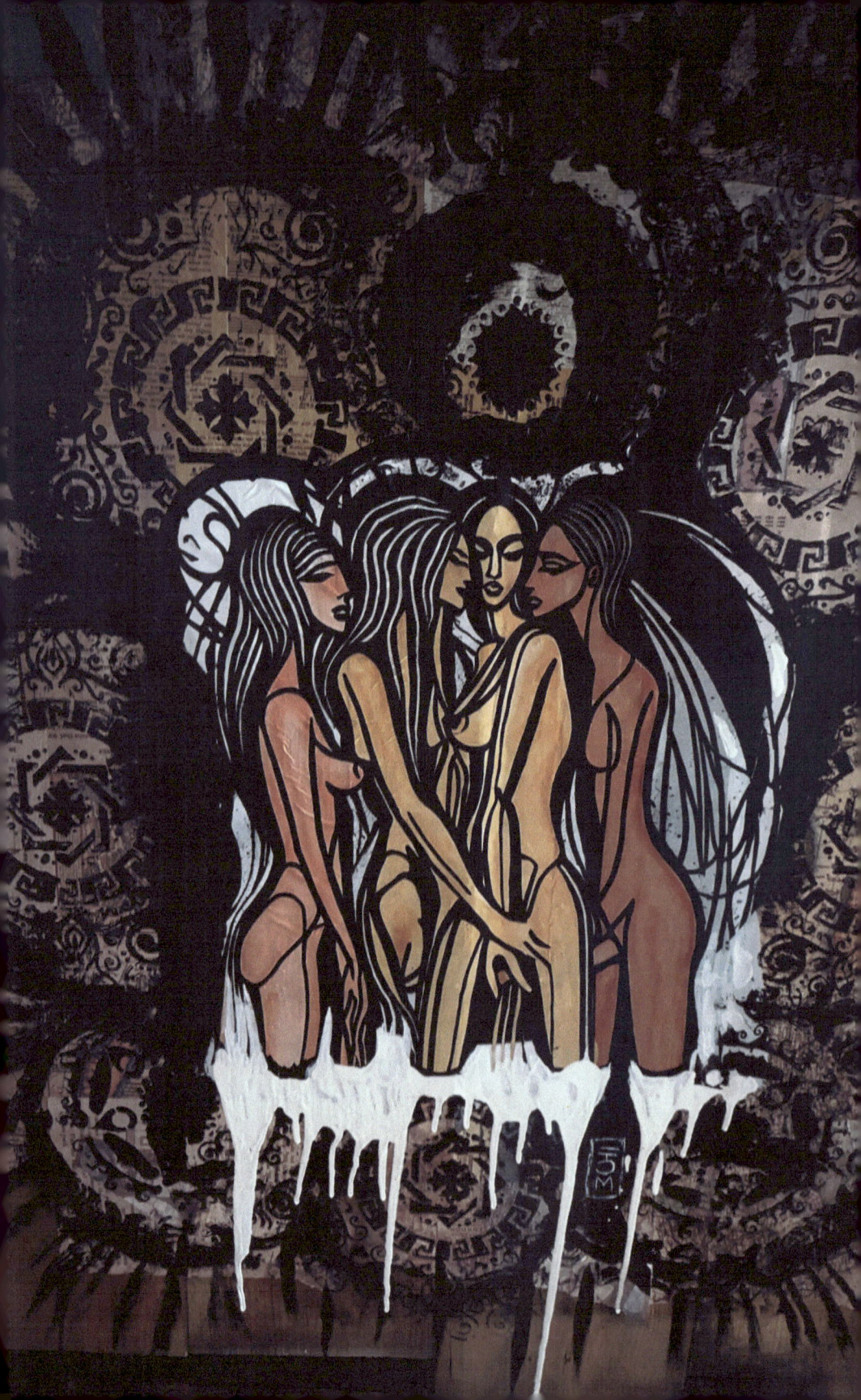

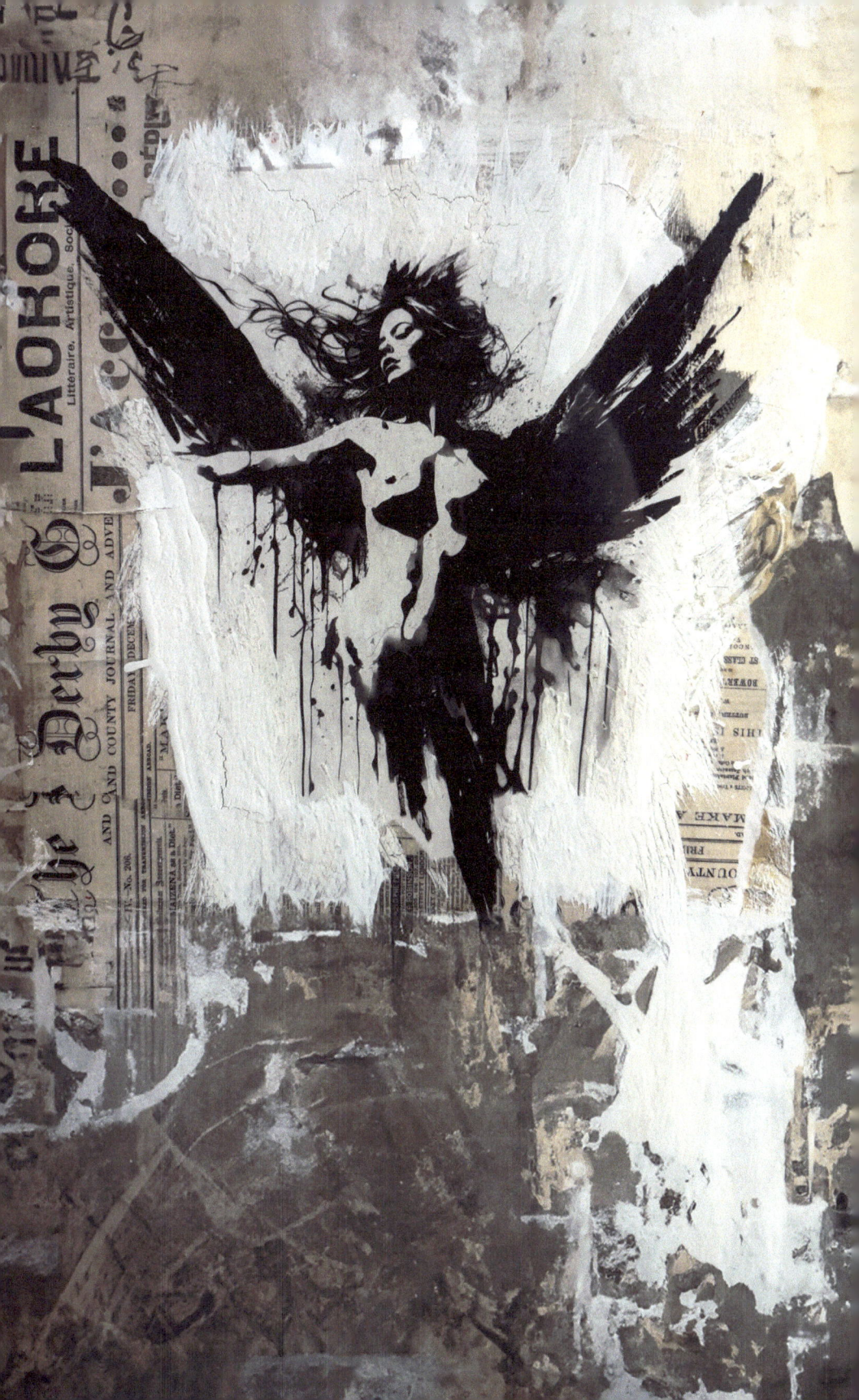

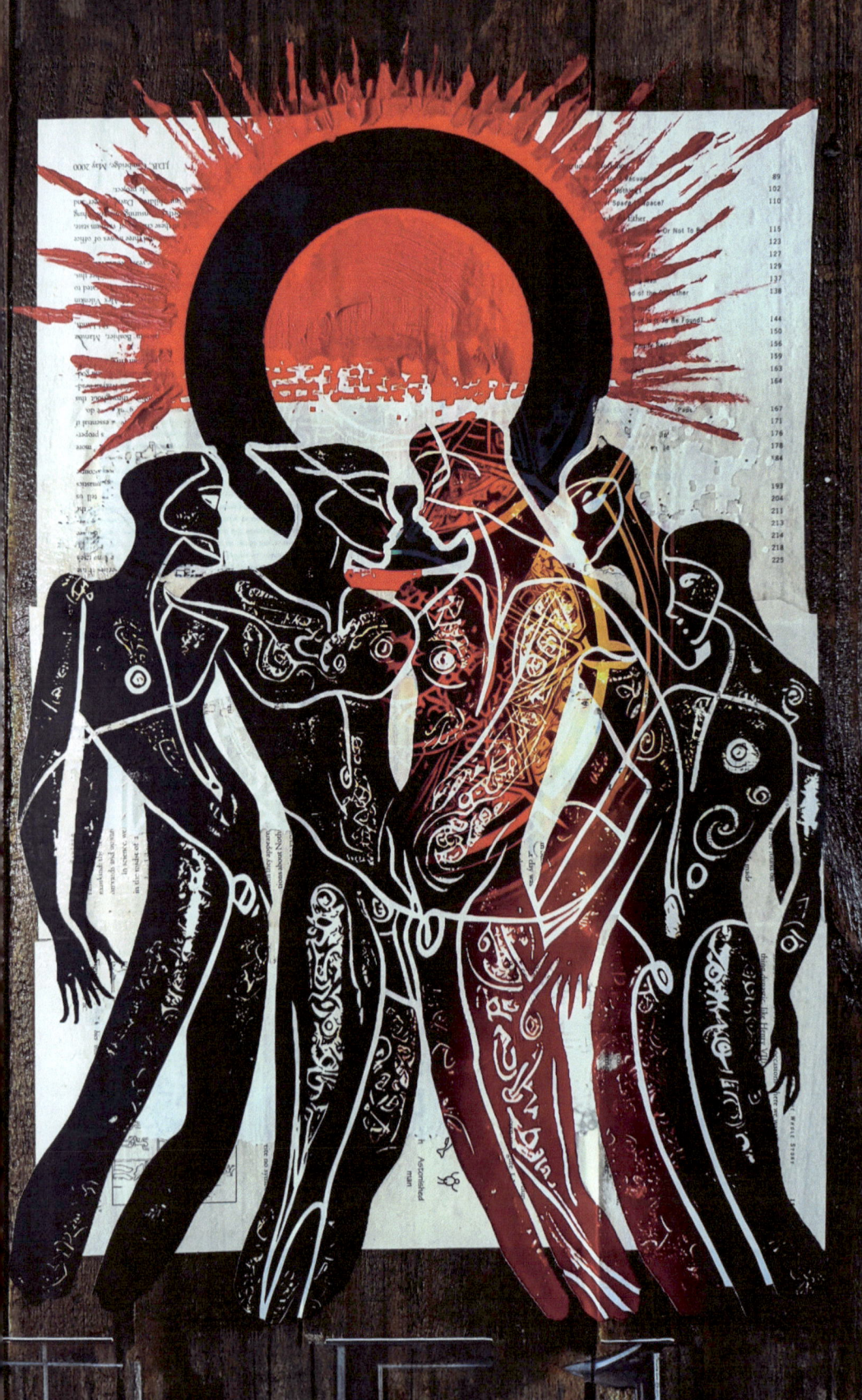

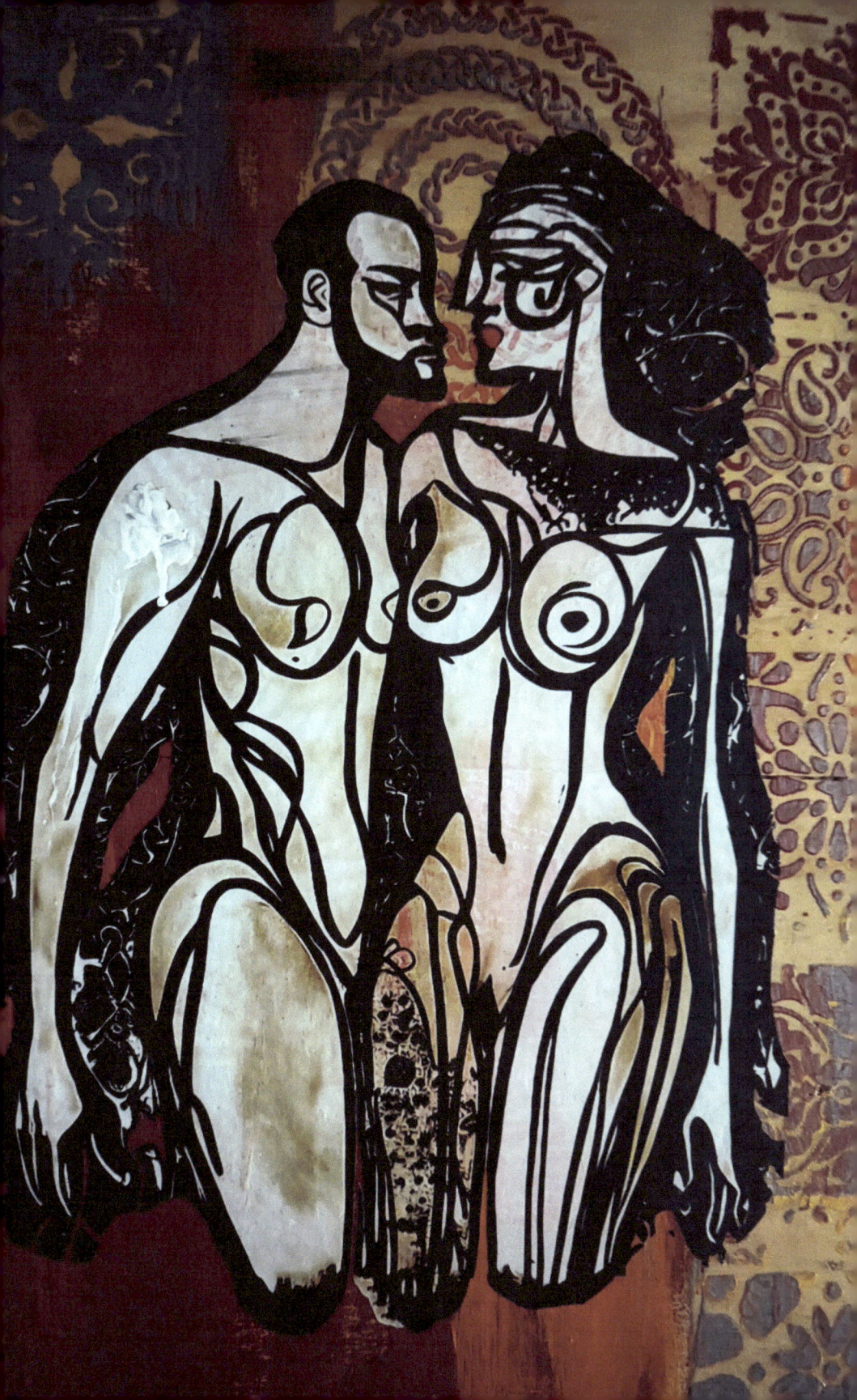

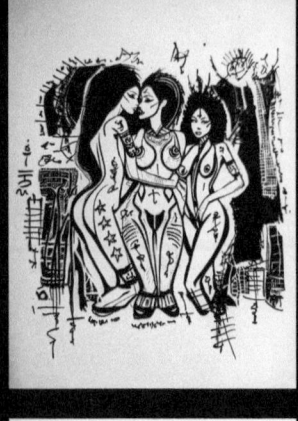
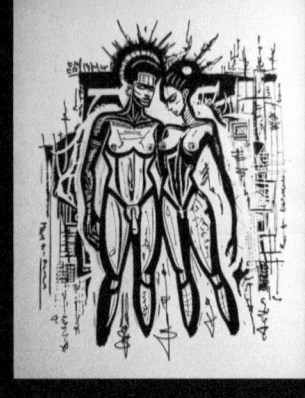
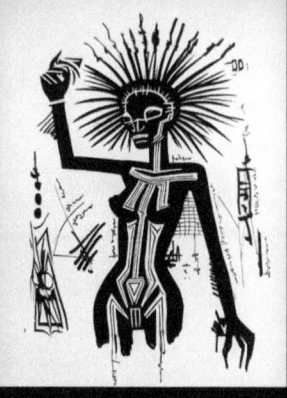
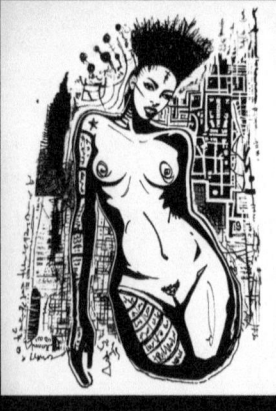
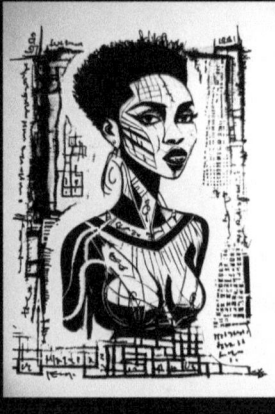
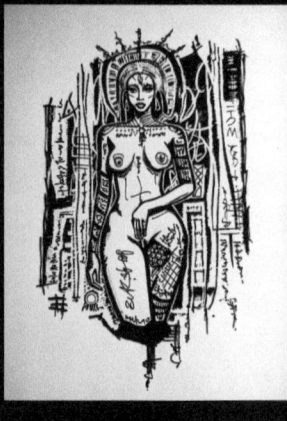

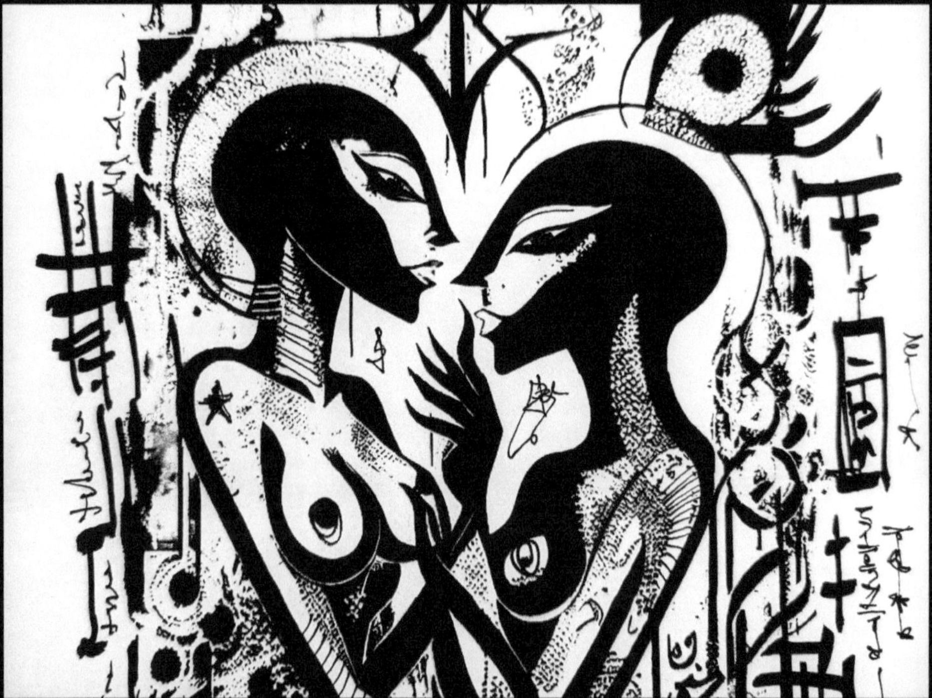

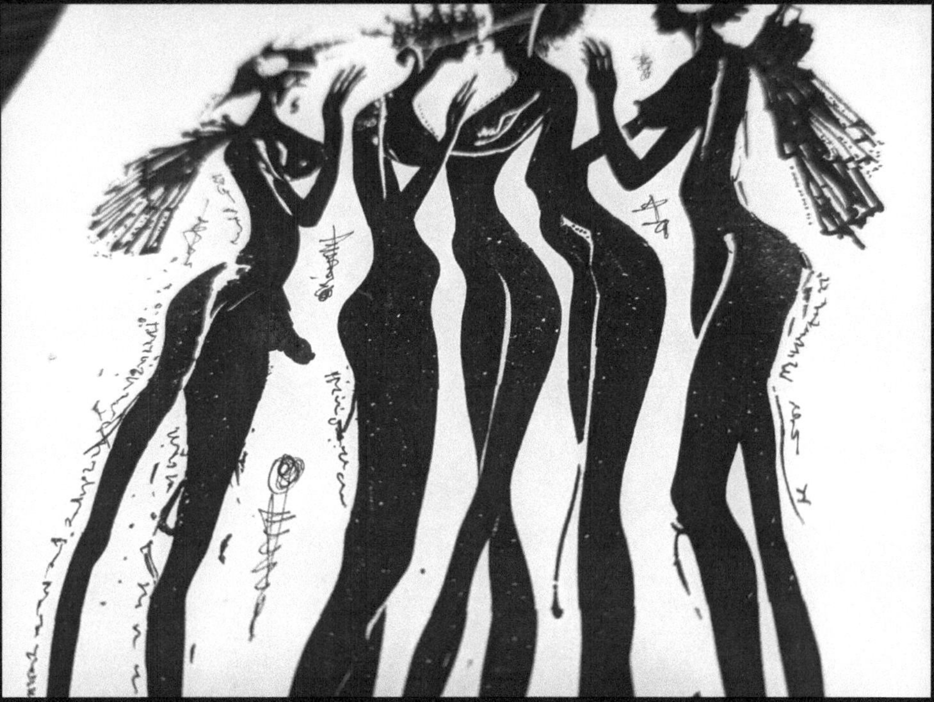

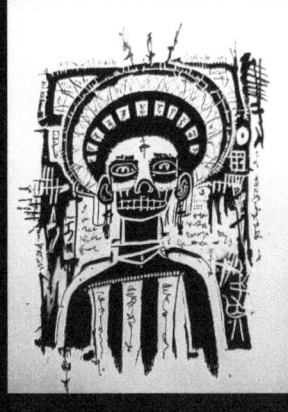
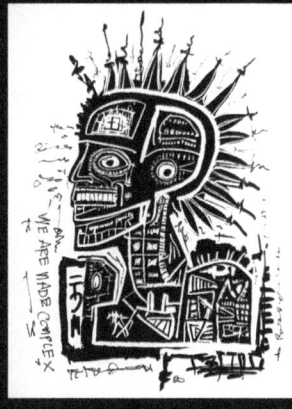
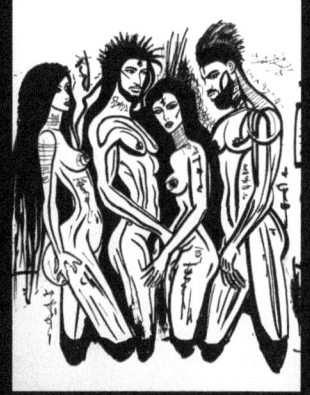
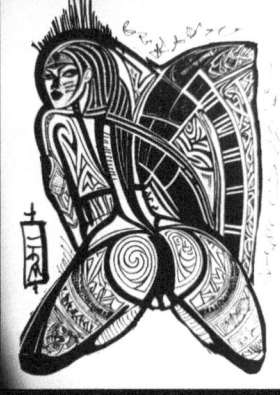
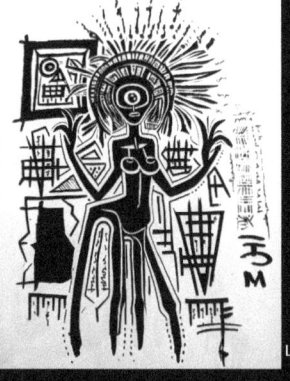
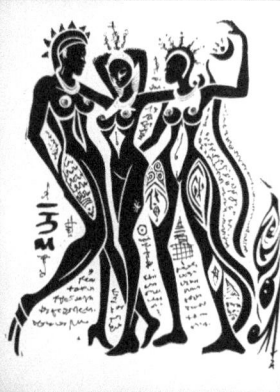

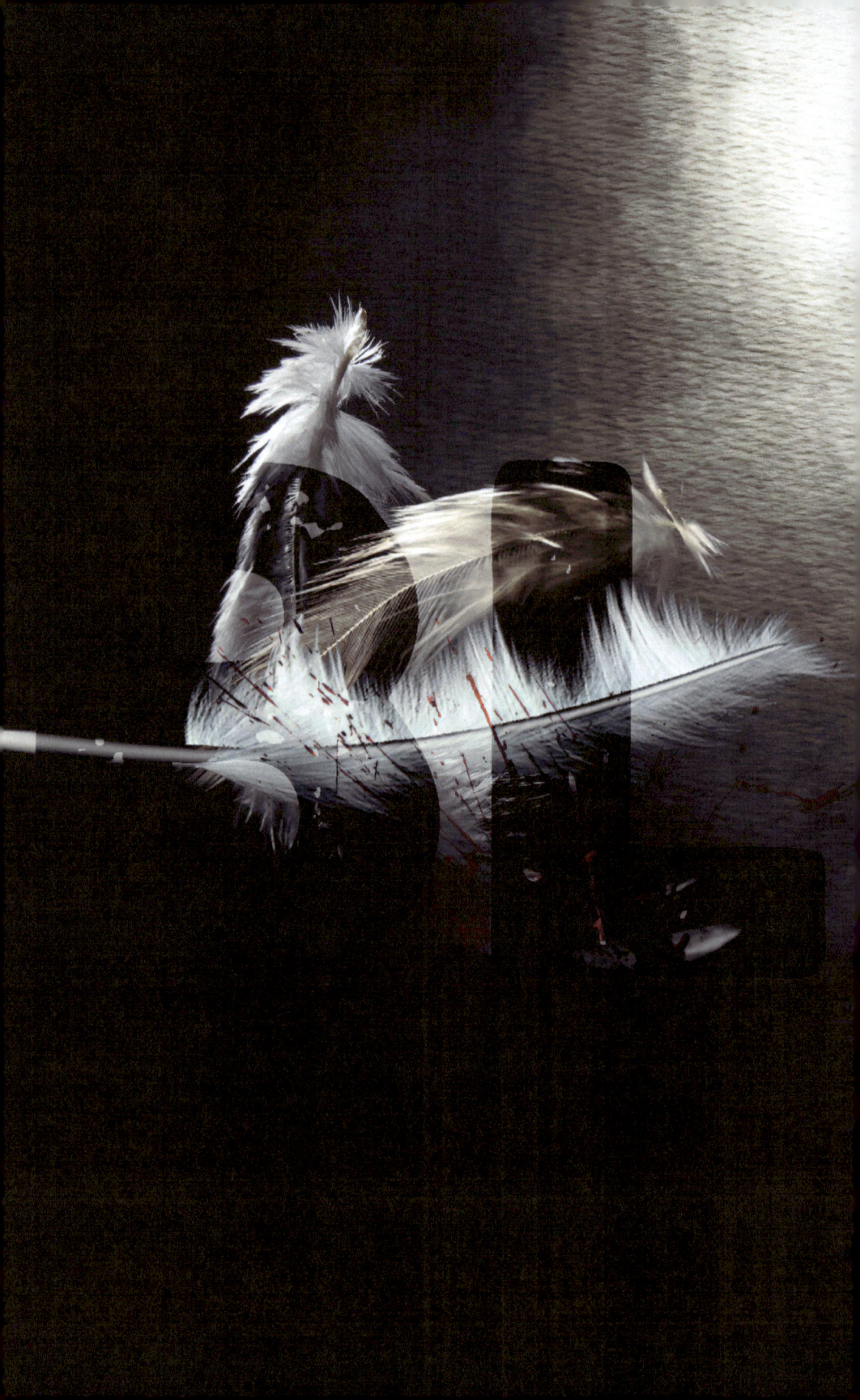

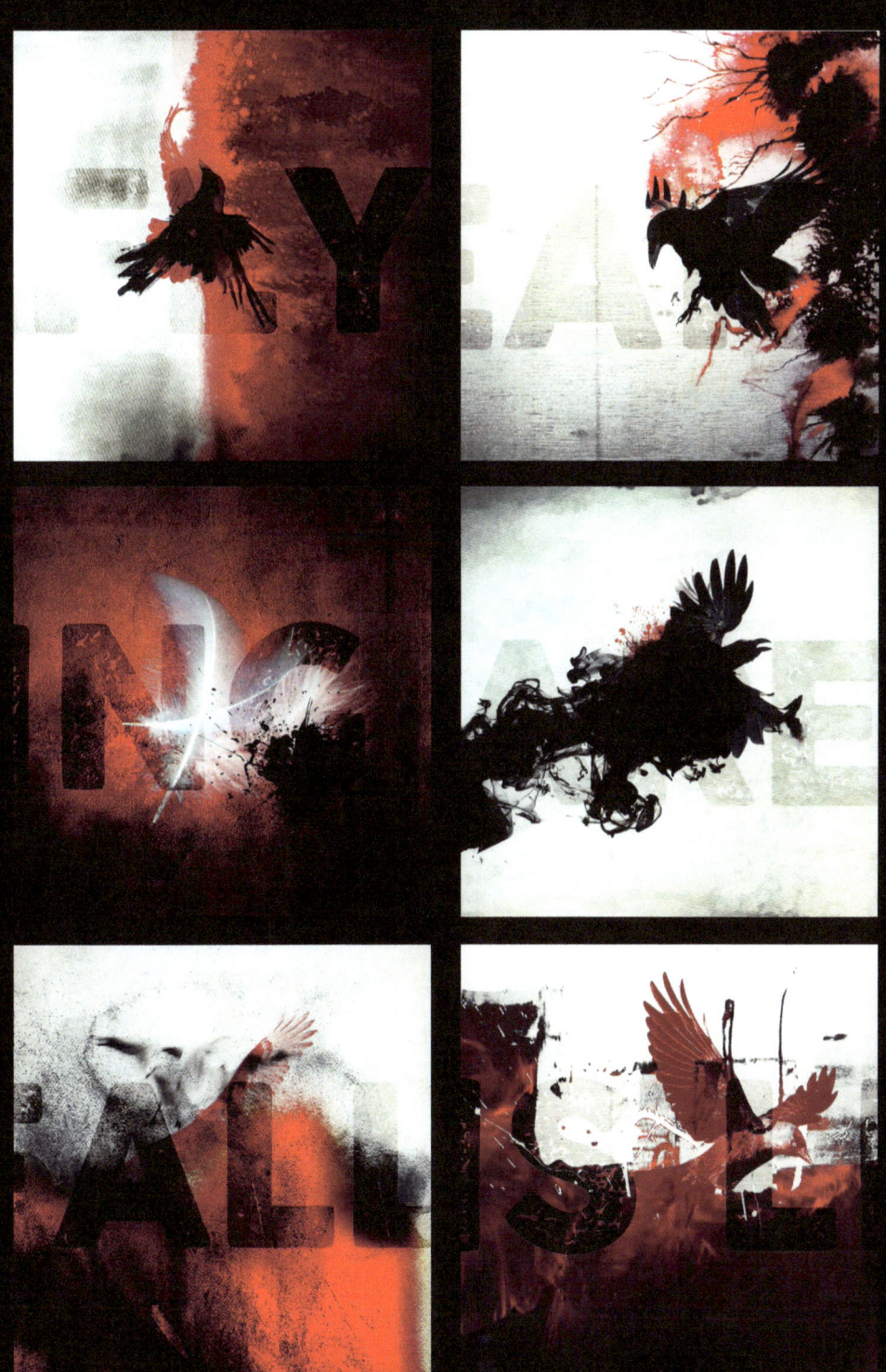

Logos

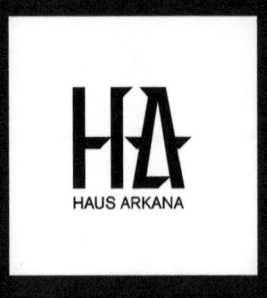

HAUS ARKANA

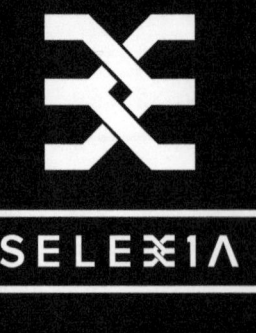

SELE⅍1Λ

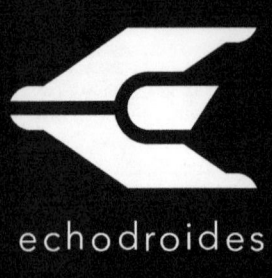

echodroides

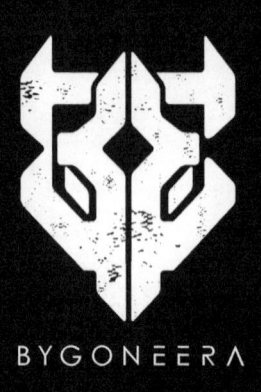

BYGONEERA

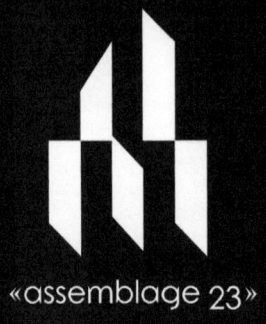

«assemblage 23»

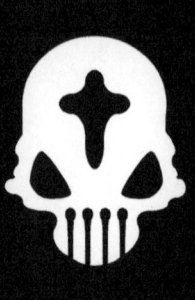

THE DEAD ROOM

RATIO STRAIN

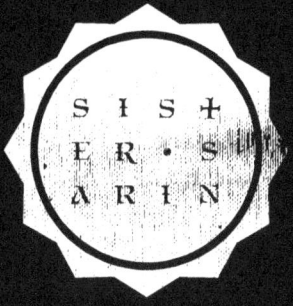

SOMETHINGCURIOUS

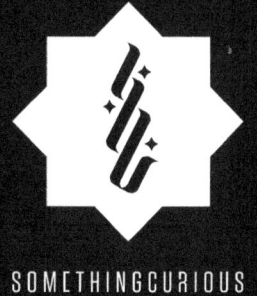

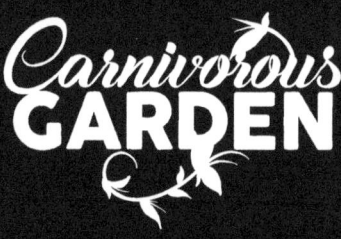

Stella Soleil

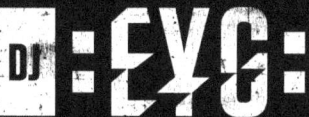

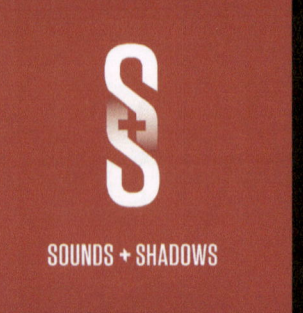

SOUNDS + SHADOWS

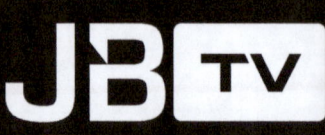

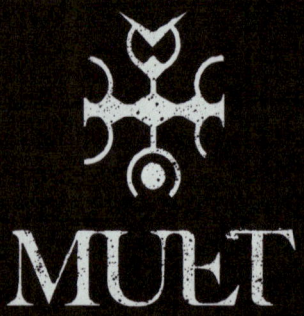

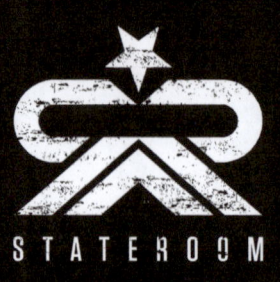

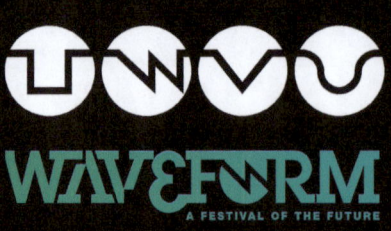

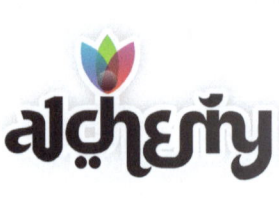

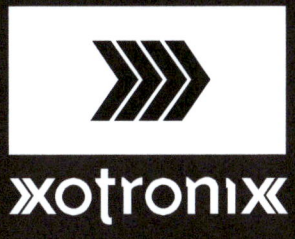

xotronix

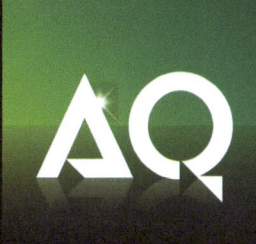

AQ

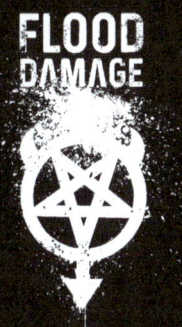

FLOOD DAMAGE

21st century burnout

DISSONANCE

PANIC UNIT

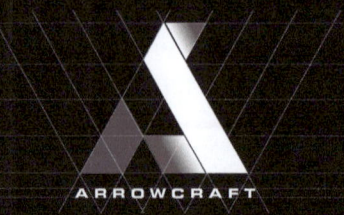

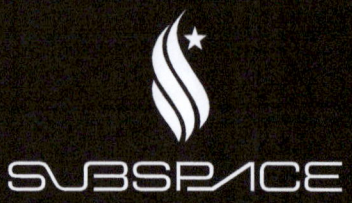

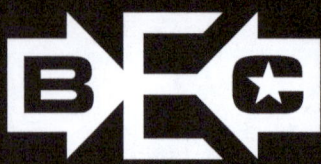

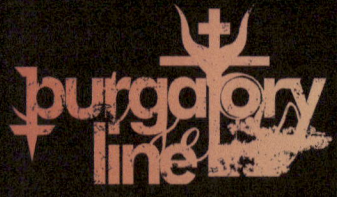

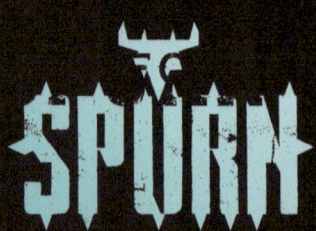

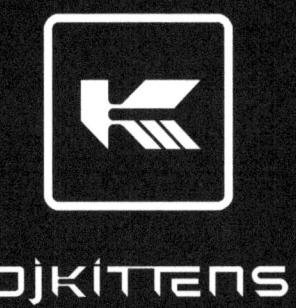

DJKITTENS

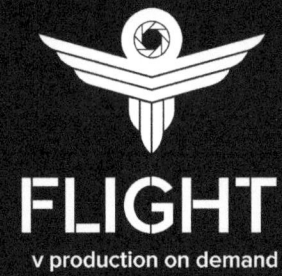

FLIGHT

v production on demand

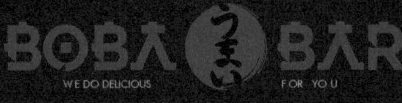

ZOLTAR

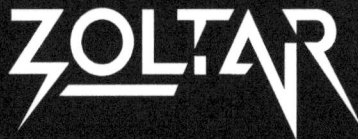

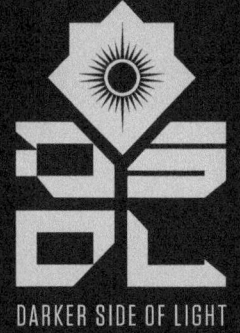

DARKER SIDE OF LIGHT

SUBROSA

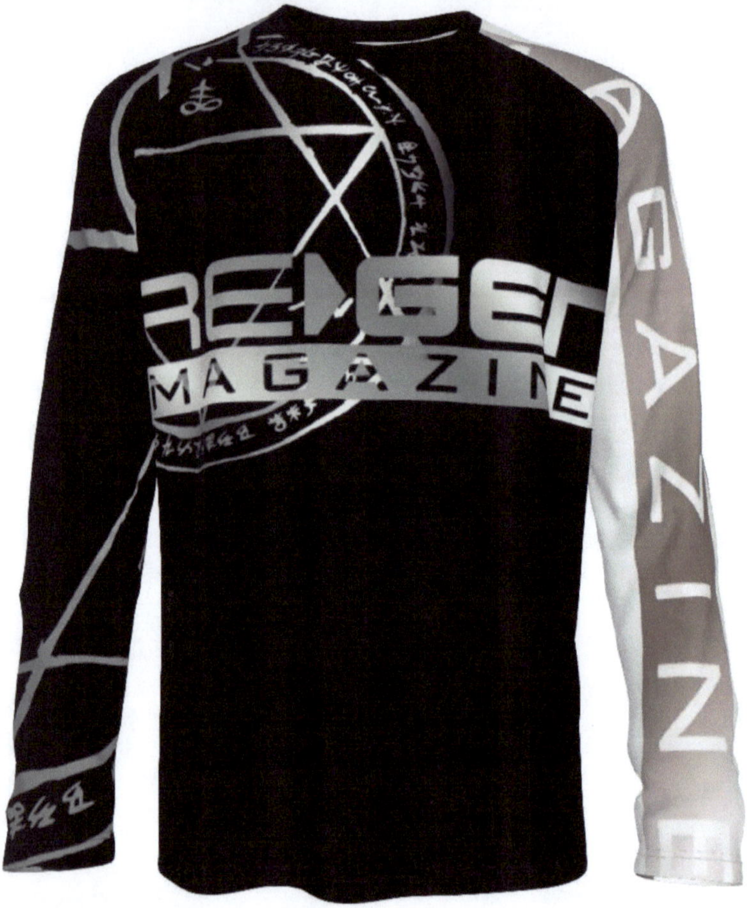

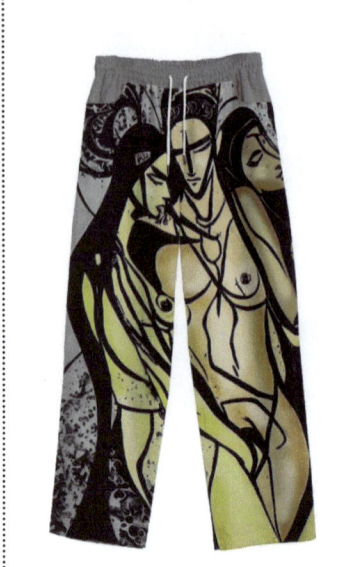
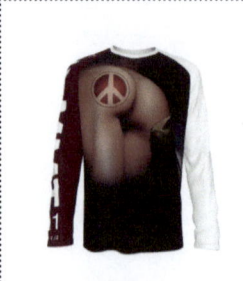
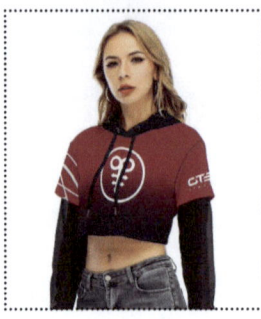
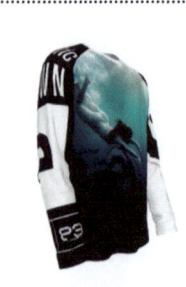
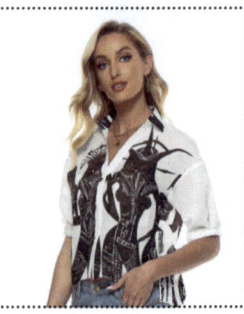

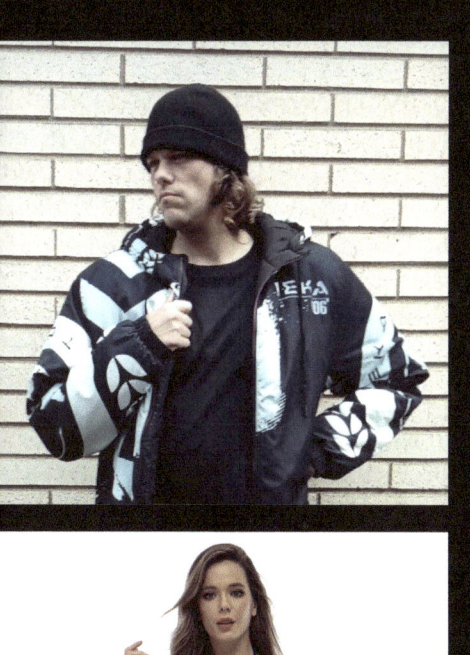
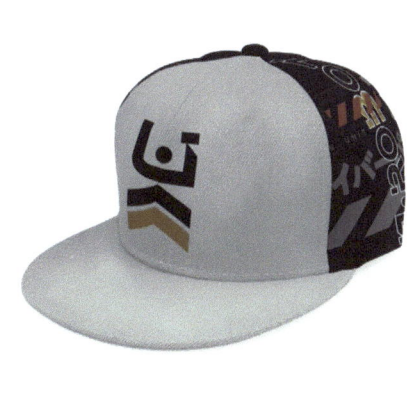
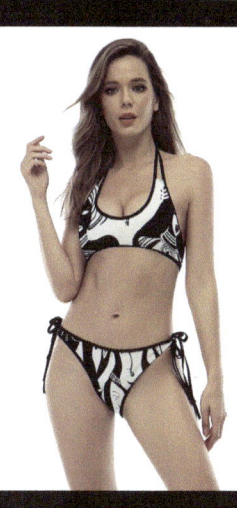
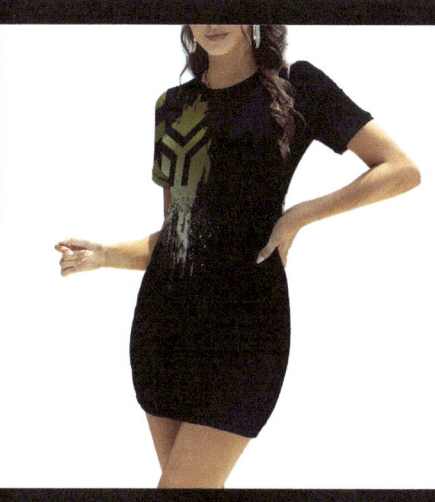
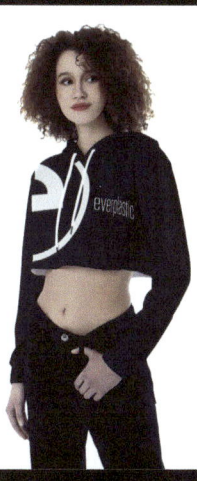
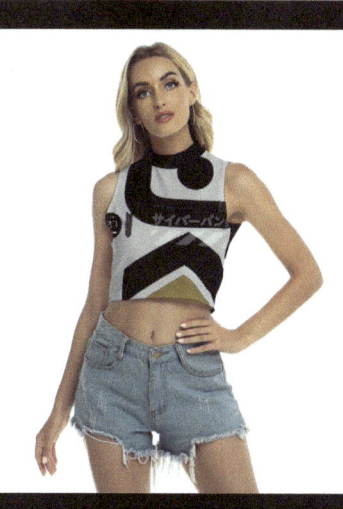

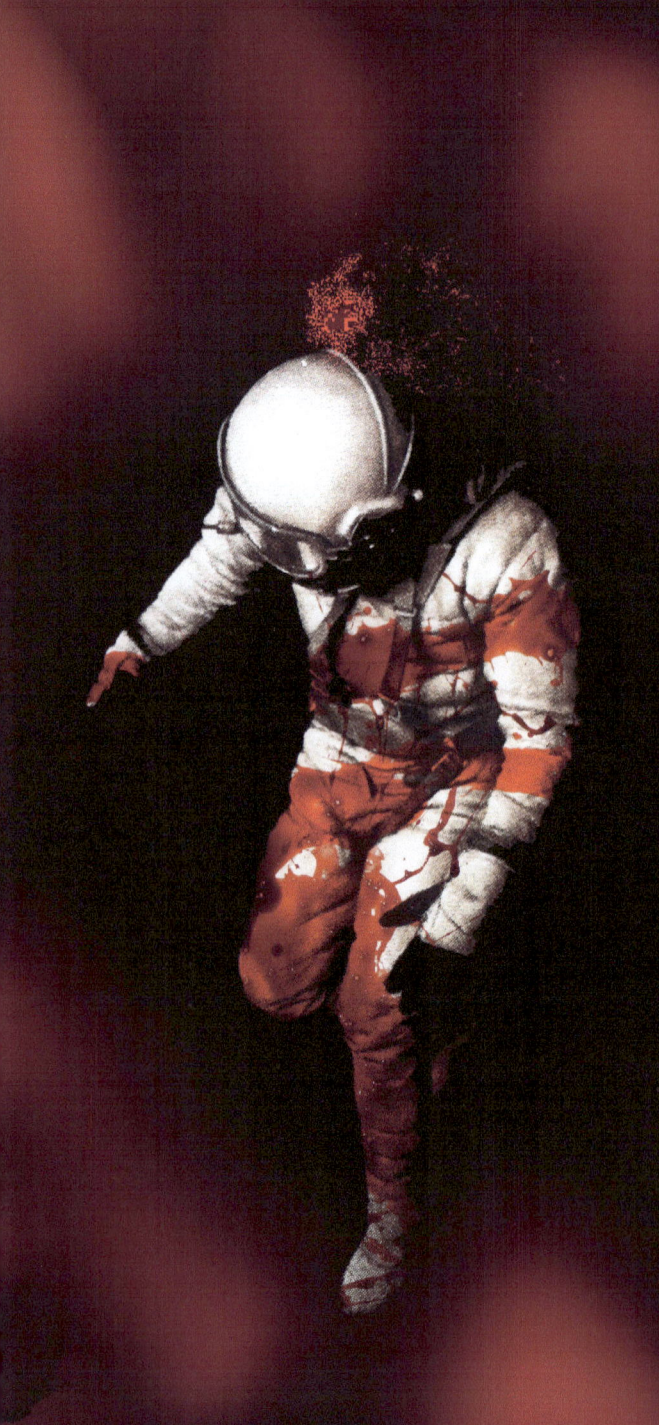

OVER ALL

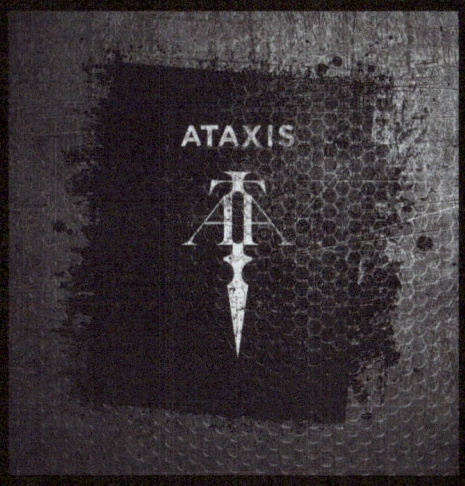

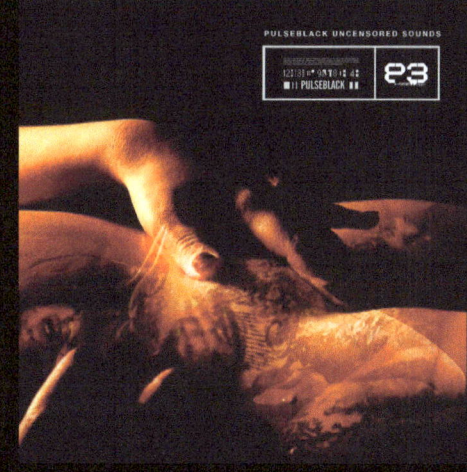

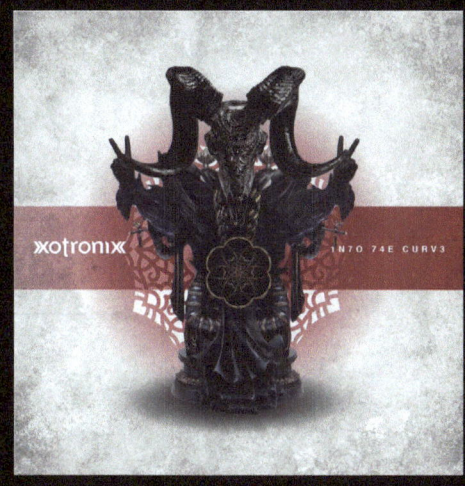

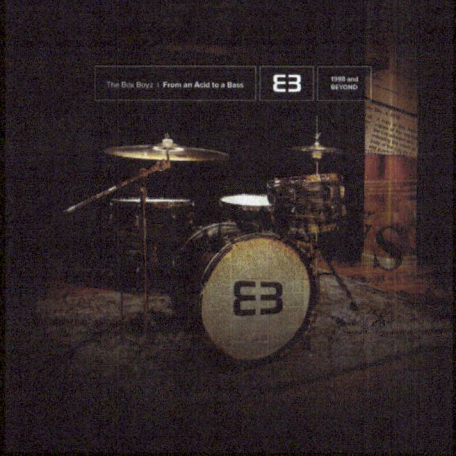

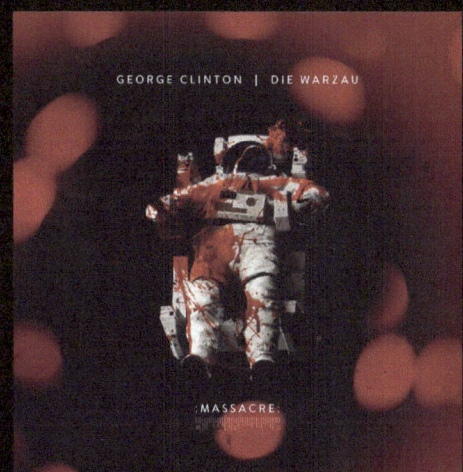

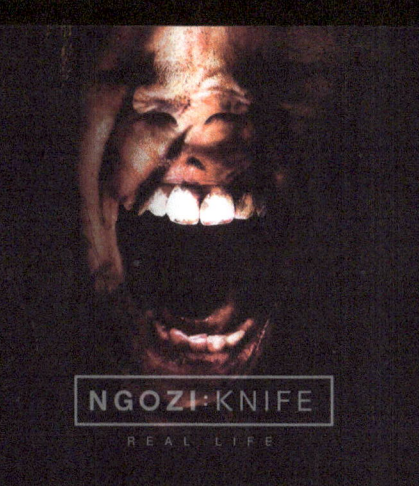

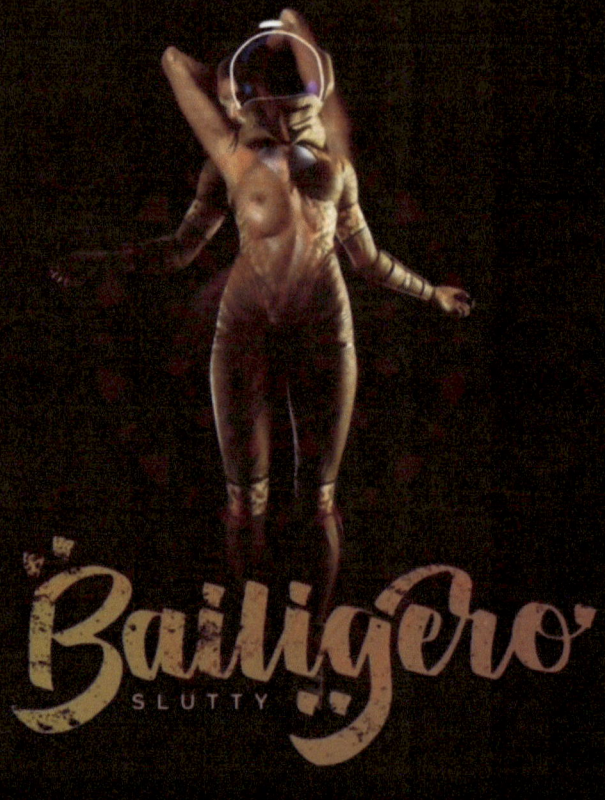

Bailigero

SLUTTY

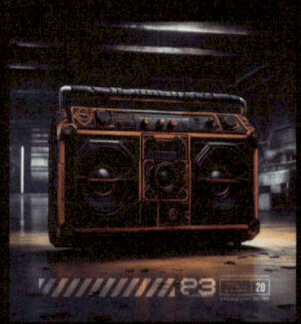
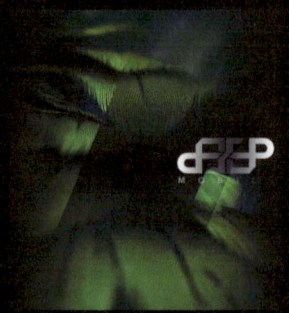
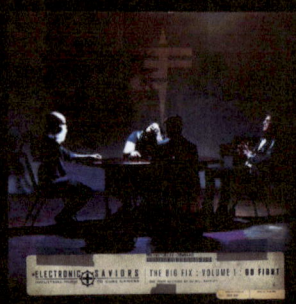
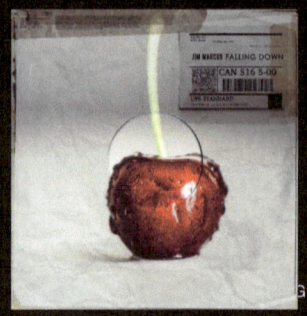
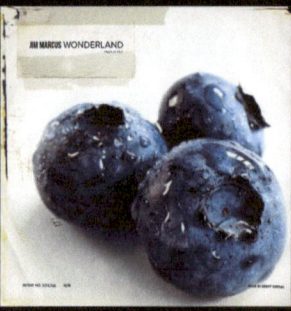
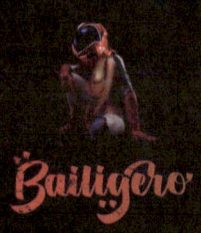

Bailigero

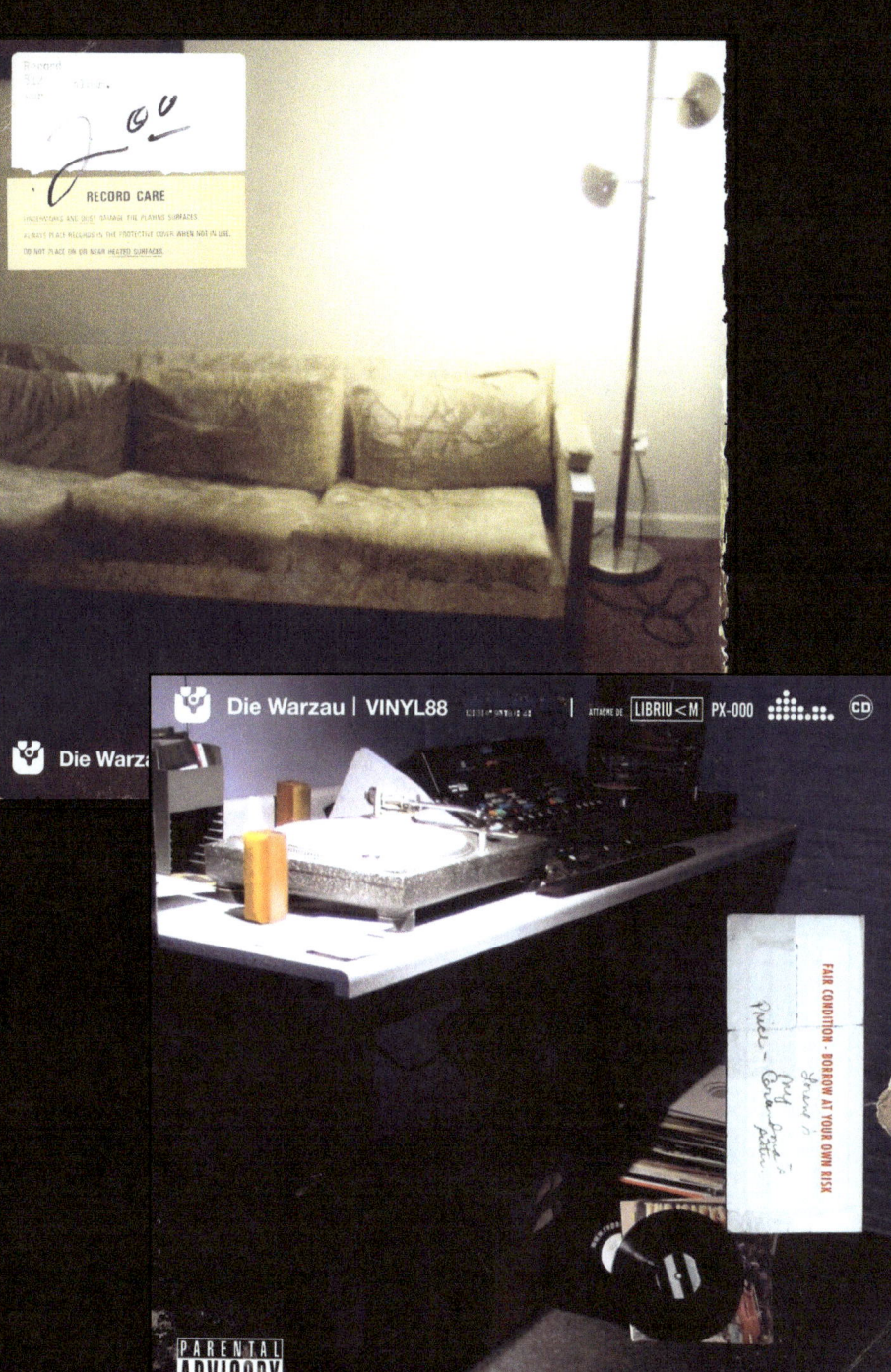

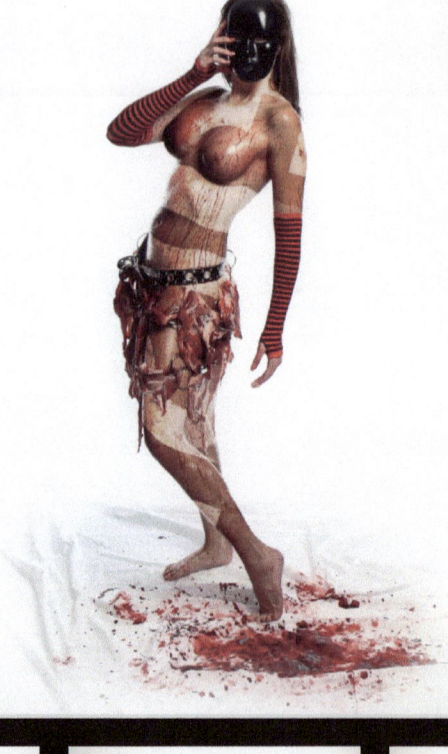

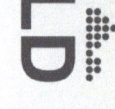

R | RESTRICTED

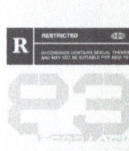

23

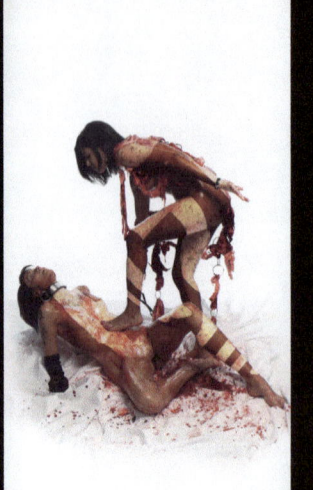

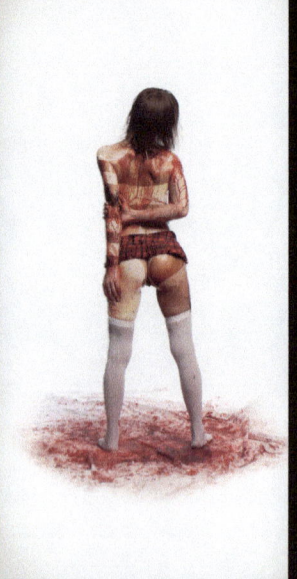

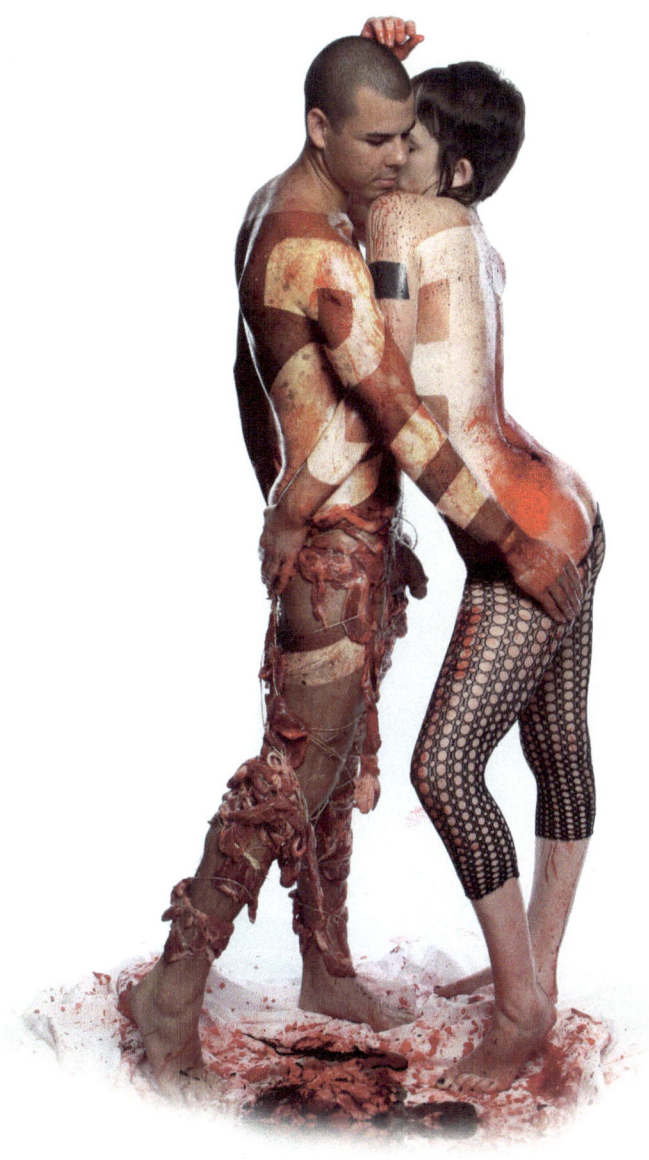

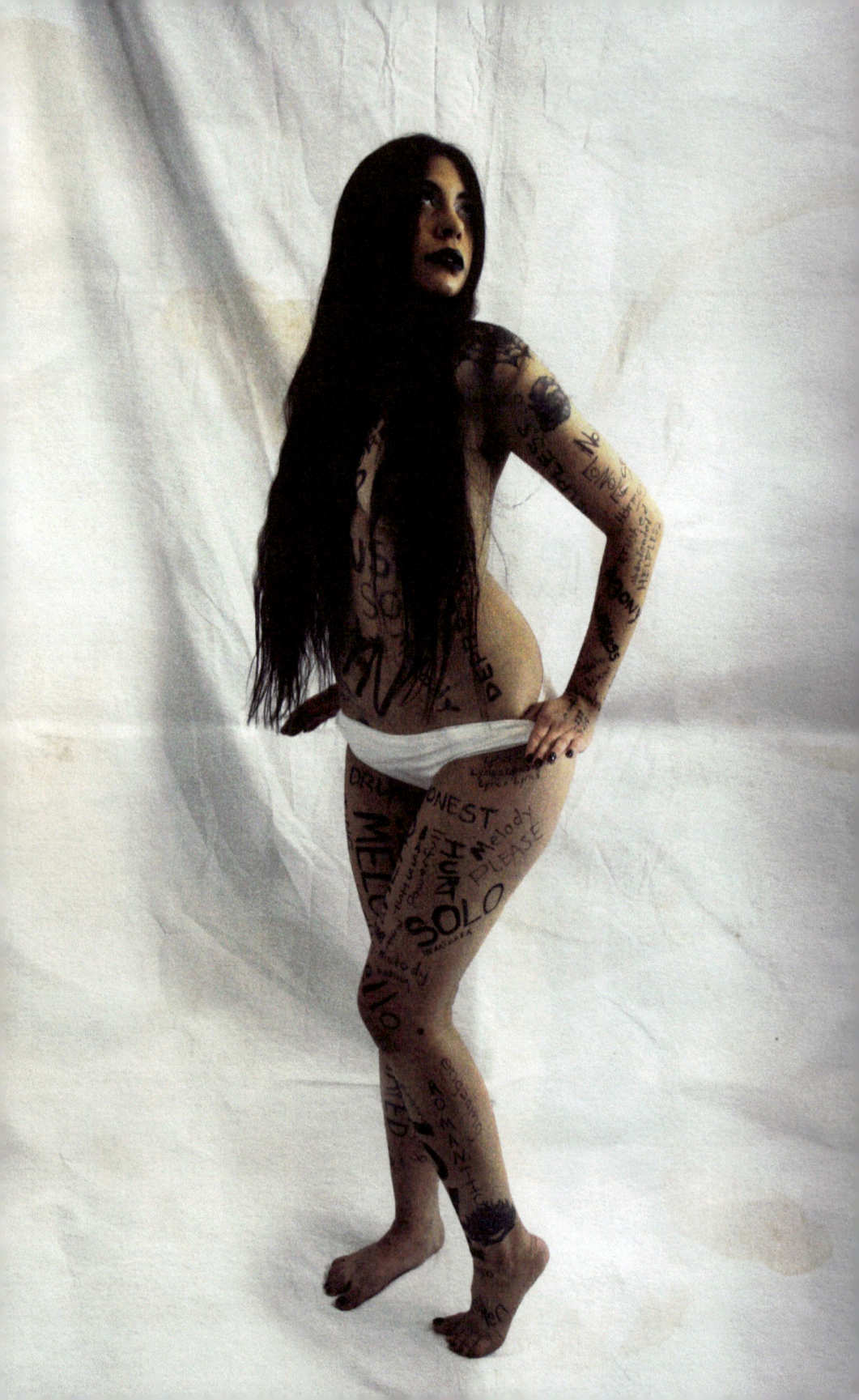

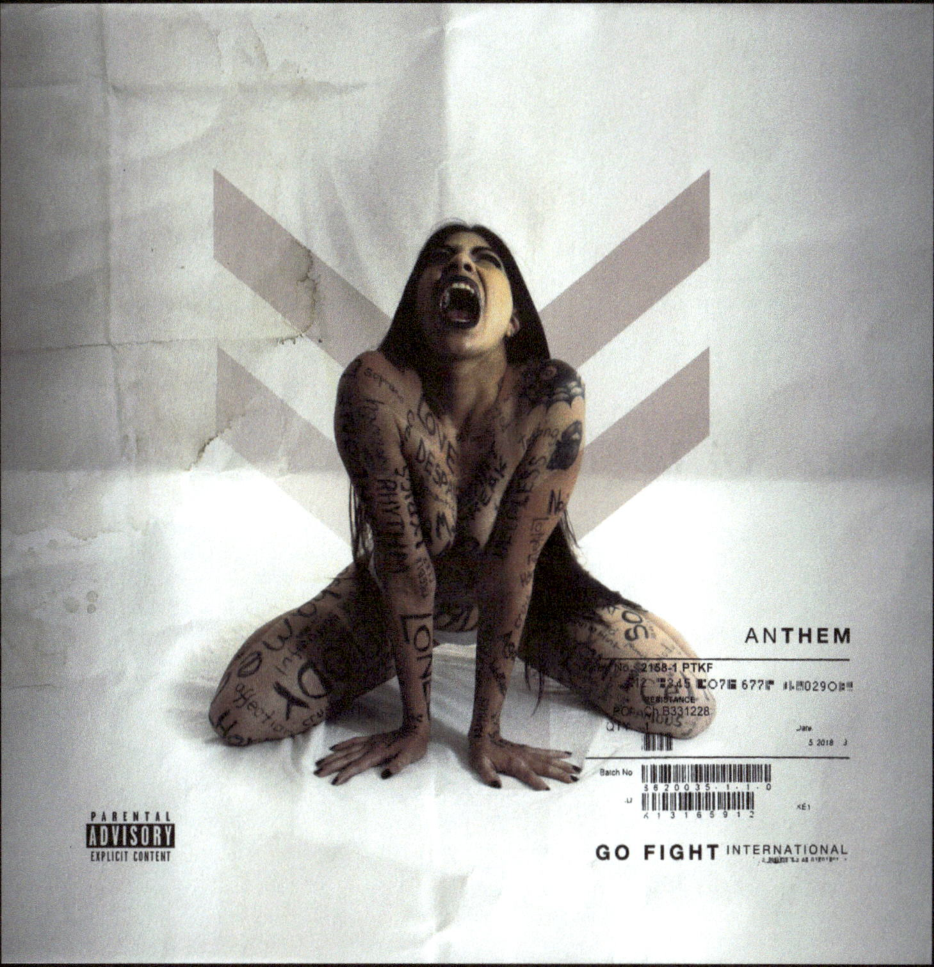

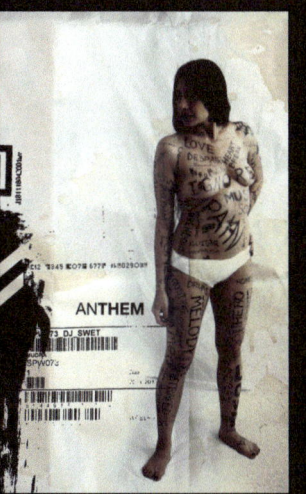
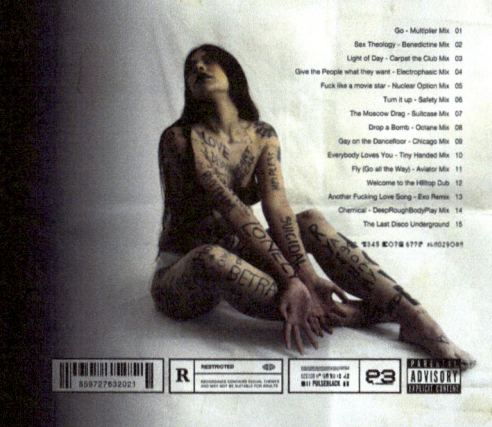

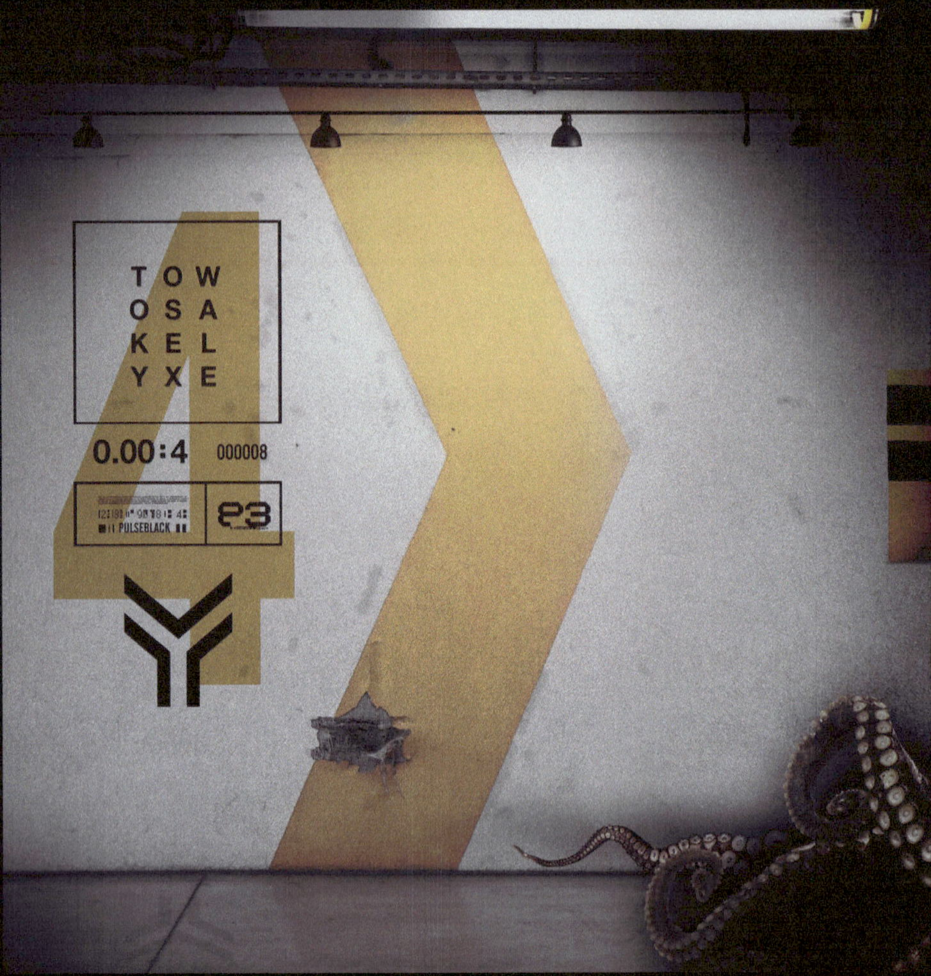

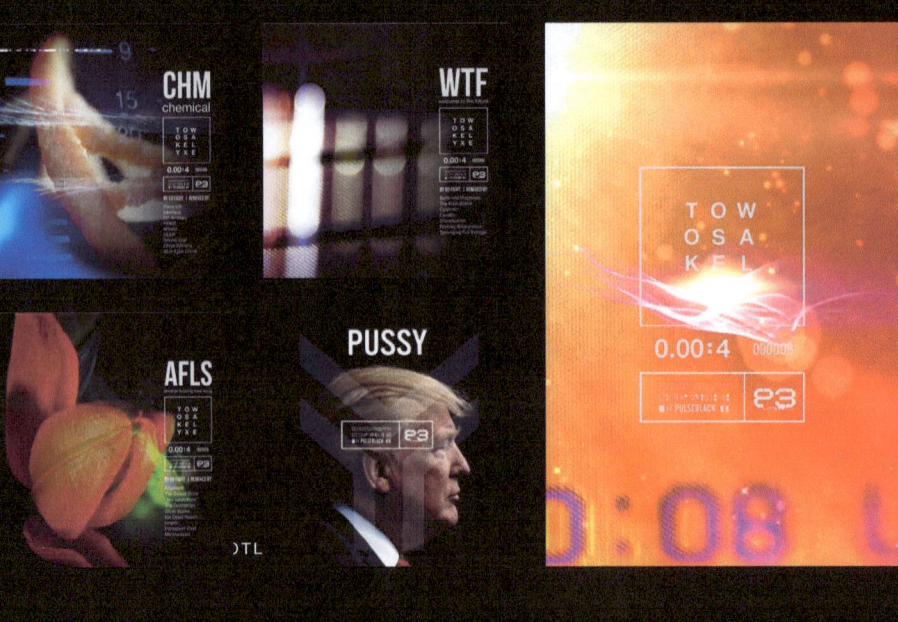

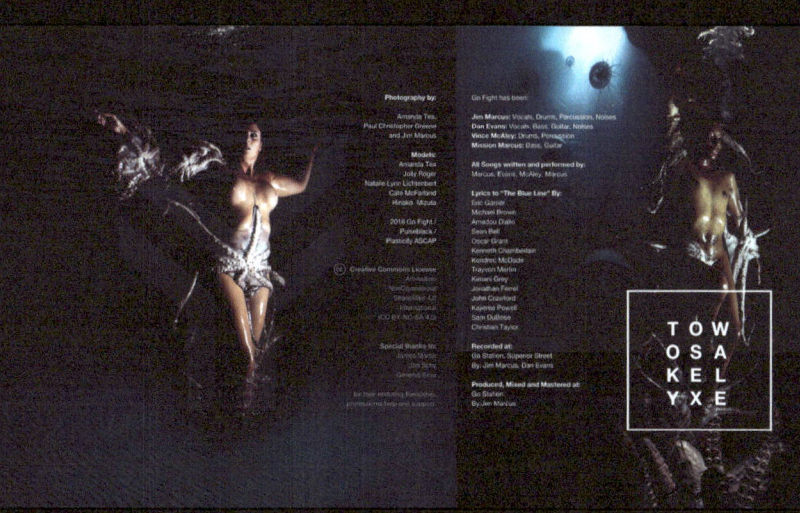

0.00:4   000008

Go Fight has been:

Jim Marcus: Vocals, Drums, Percussion, Noises
Dan Evans: Vocals, Bass, Guitar, Noises
Vince McAley: Drums, Percussion
Mission Marcus: Bass, Guitar

All Songs written and performed by:
Marcus, Evans, McAley, Marcus

Lyrics to "The Blue Line" By:
Eric Garner
Michael Brown
Amadou Diallo
Sean Bell
Oscar Grant
Kenneth Chamberlain
Kendrec McDade
Trayvon Martin
Kimani Grey
Jonathan Ferrel
John Crawford
Kajieme Powell
Sam Dubose
Christian Taylor

Recorded at:
Go Station, Superior Street
By: Jim Marcus, Dan Evans

Produced, Mixed and Mastered at:
Go Station
By: Jim Marcus

Photography by:

Amanda Tixi,
Paul Christopher Greene
and Jim Marcus

Models:
Amanda Tixi
Jolly Roger
Natalie Lynn Lichtenbert
Cafe McFarland
Hiroko Mizuta

2016 Go Fight /
Pulseblack /
Plastically ASCAP

Special thanks to:
James Marcus
Jim Sorg
General Bitch

for their continuing friendship,
professional help and support

TO OW
OS SA
KE EL
YX XE

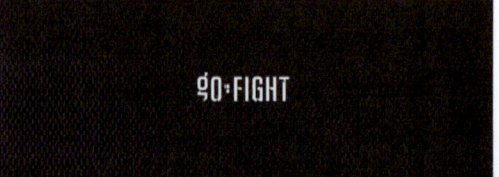

GO:FIGHT

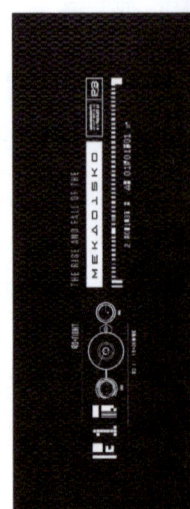

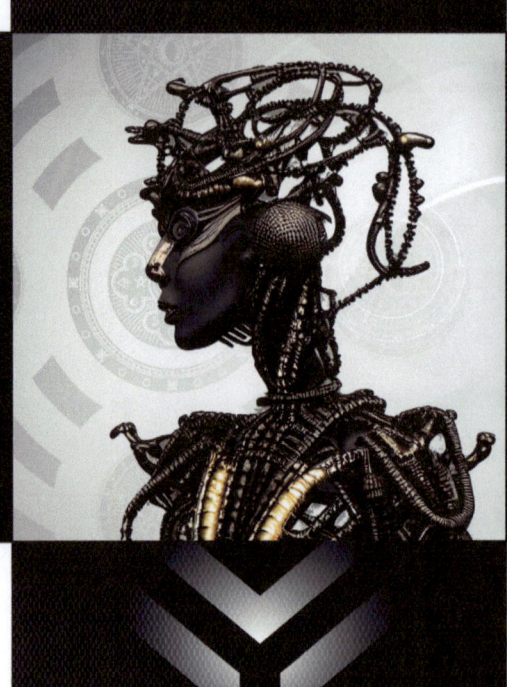

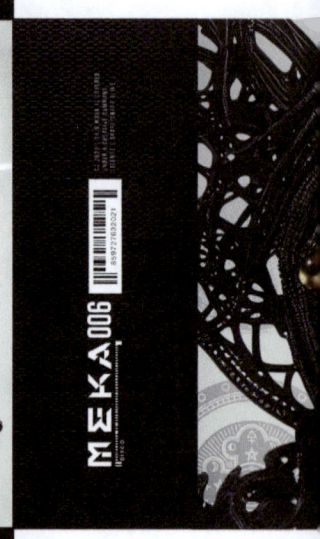

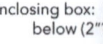

Enclosing box:
below (2"

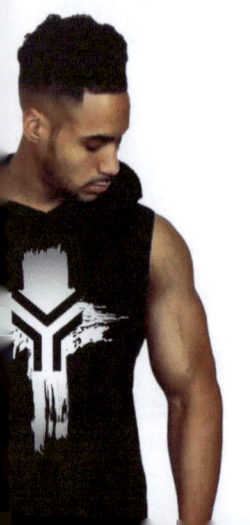

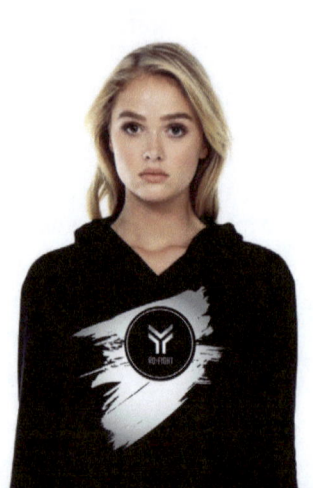

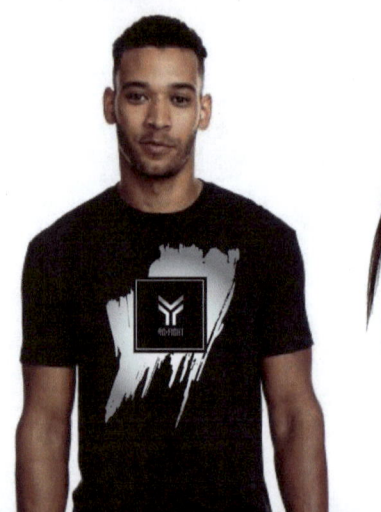

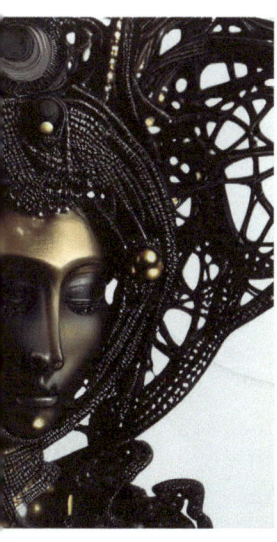

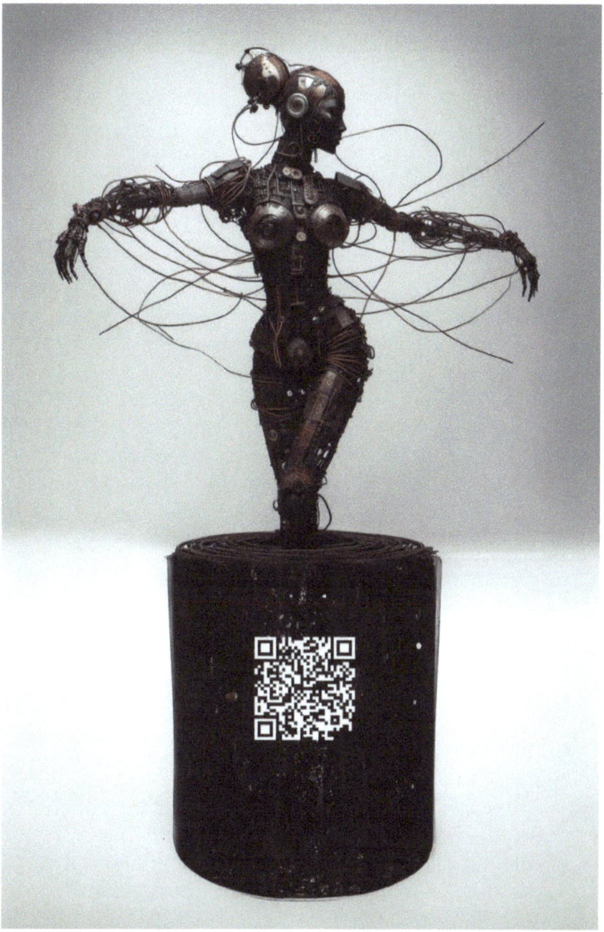

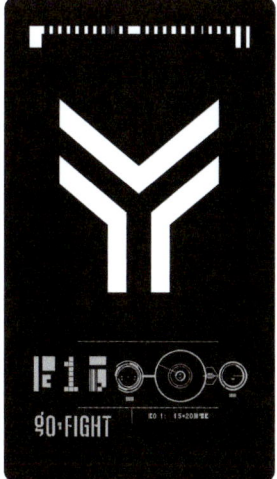

1.ENCLOSING BOX

x5" interior, cardstock, depth to fit contents
spot gloss / matte lam, inside black matte.

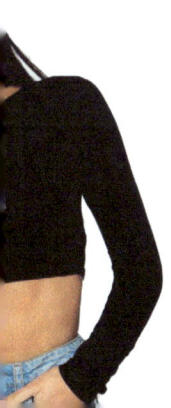

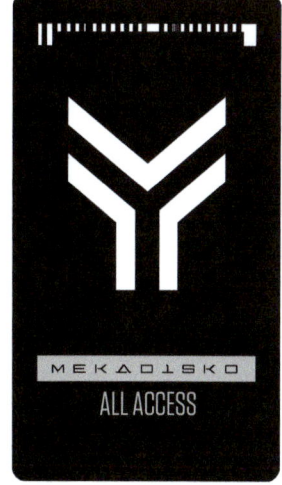

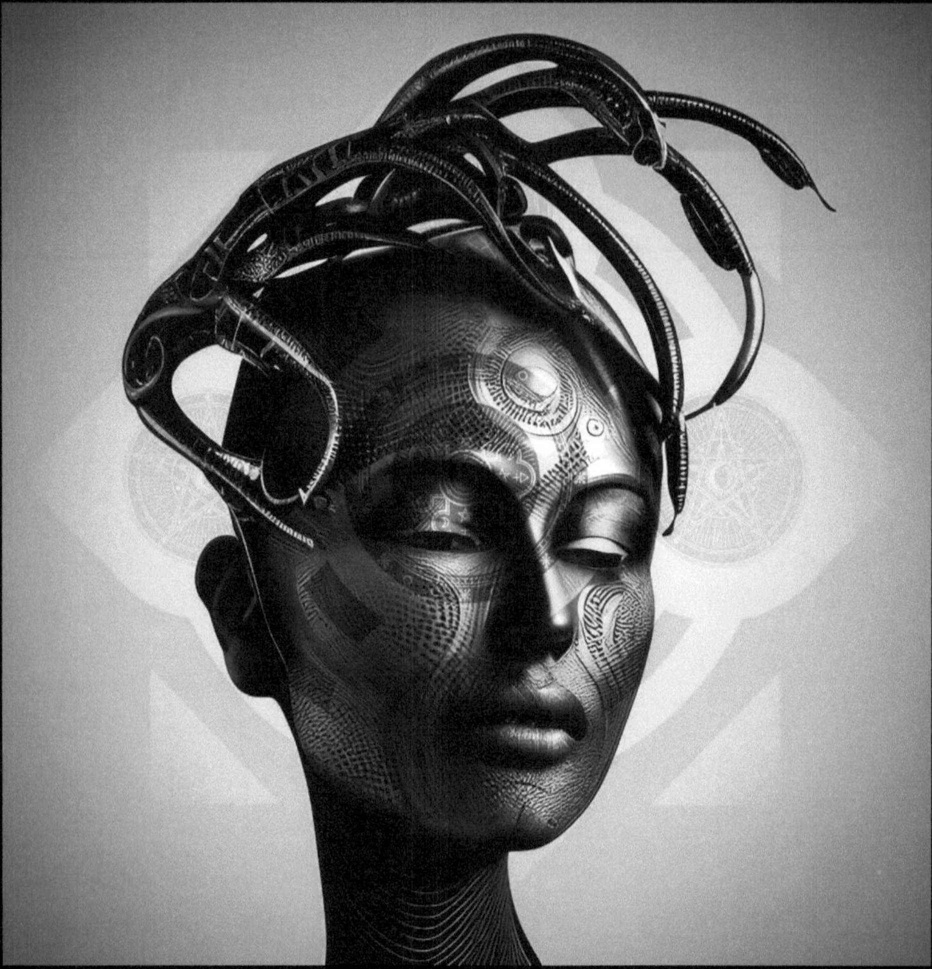

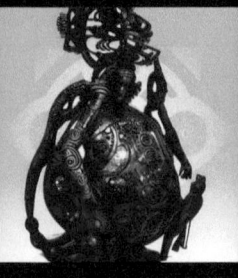
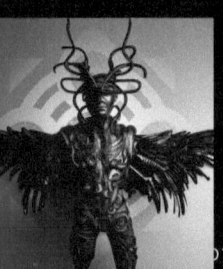
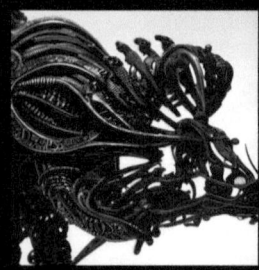
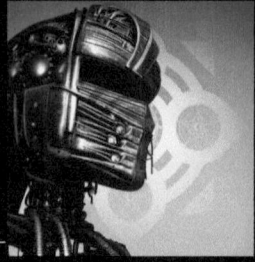
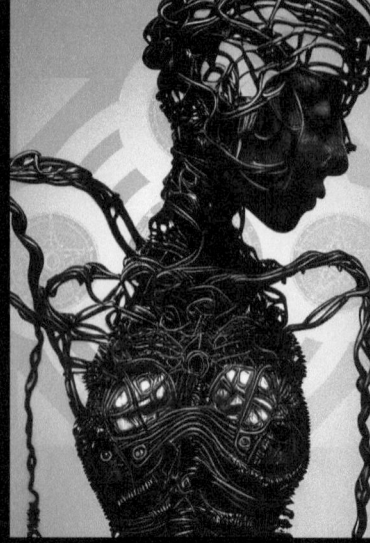

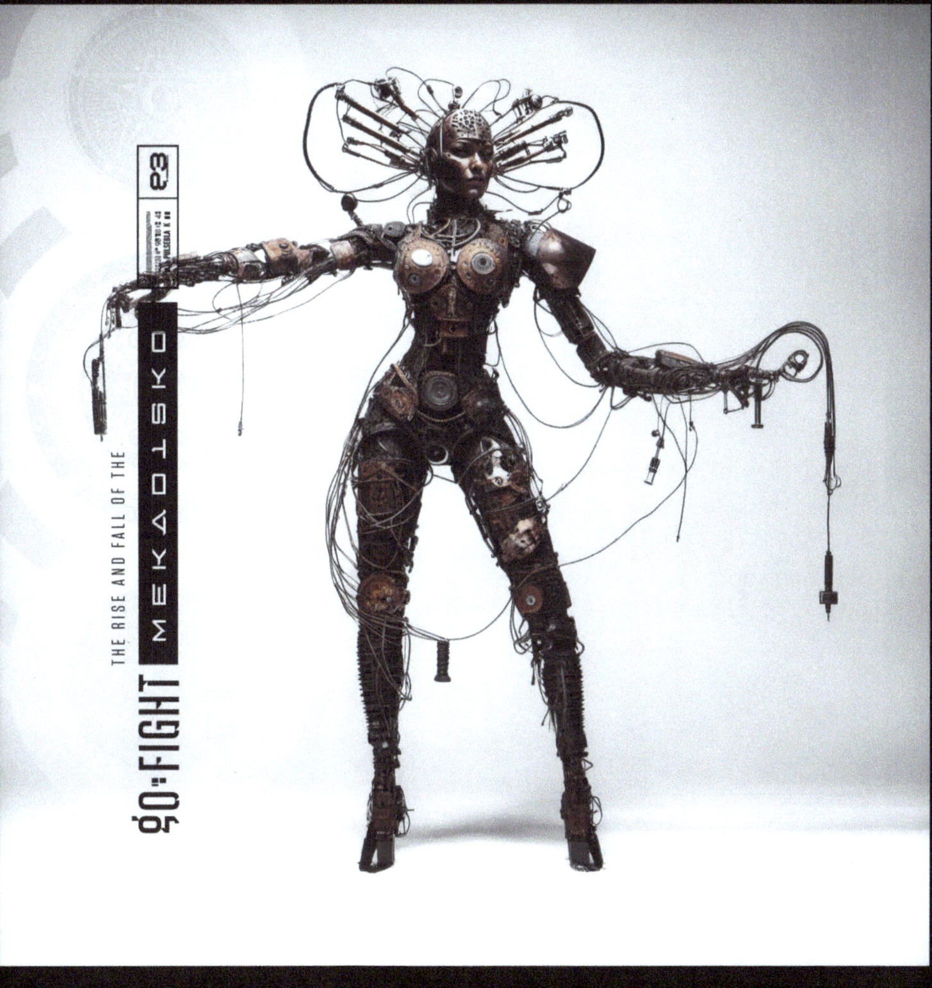

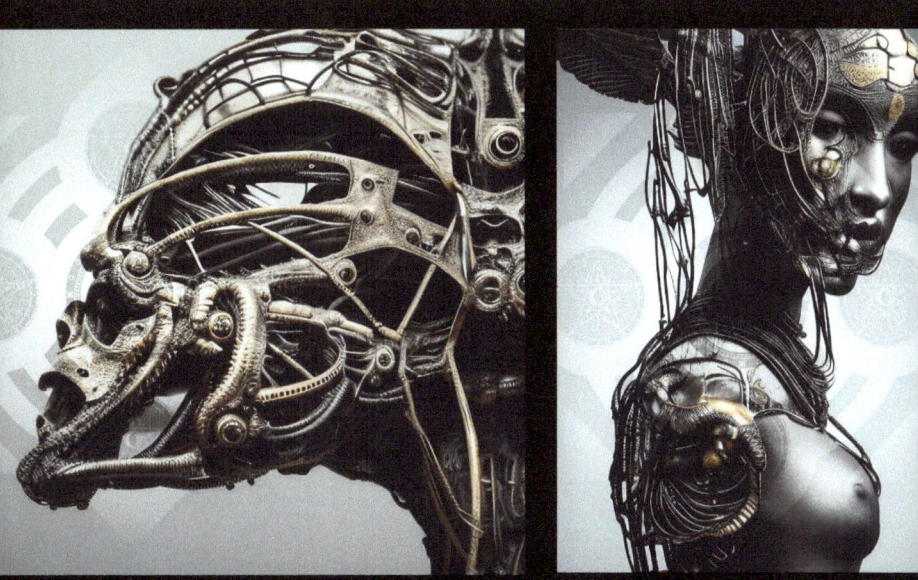

23

GO-FIGHT

THE RISE AND FALL OF THE

MEKA TOSKO

Books

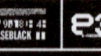

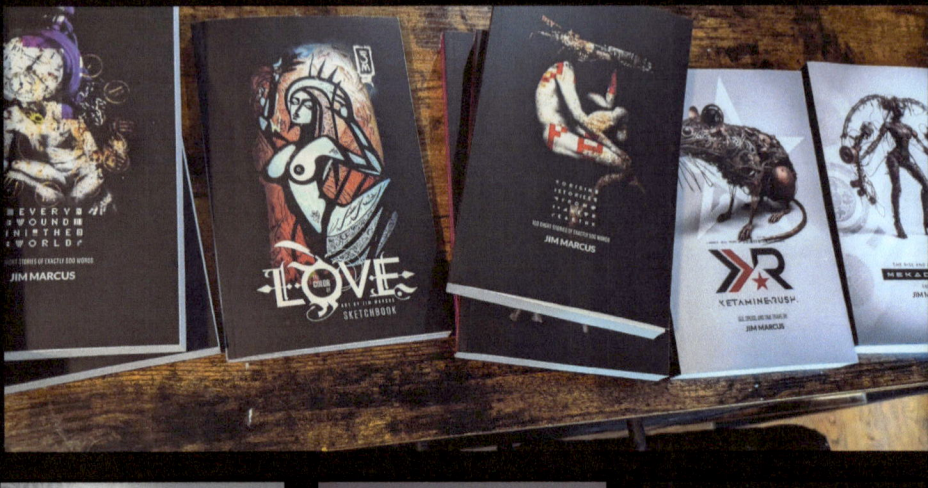

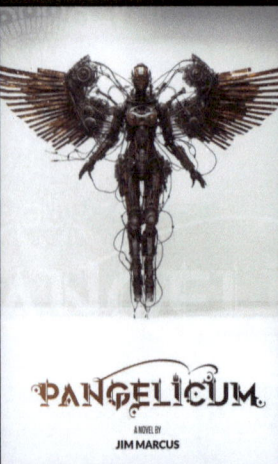

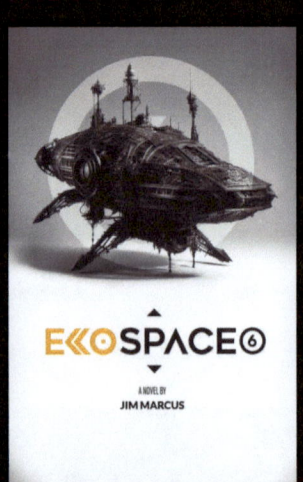

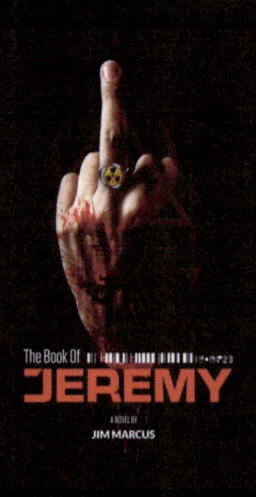

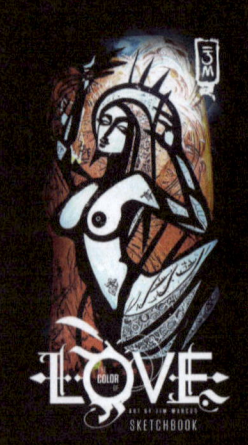

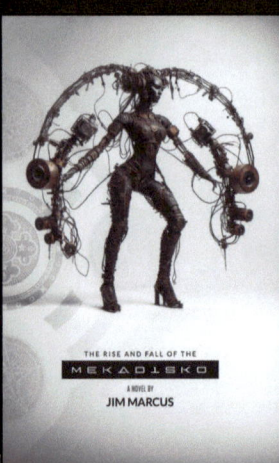

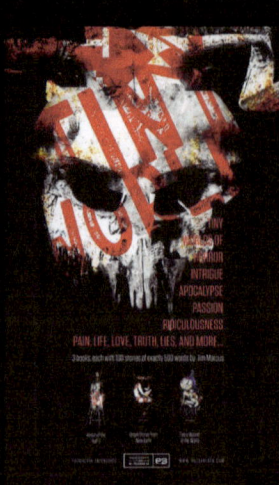

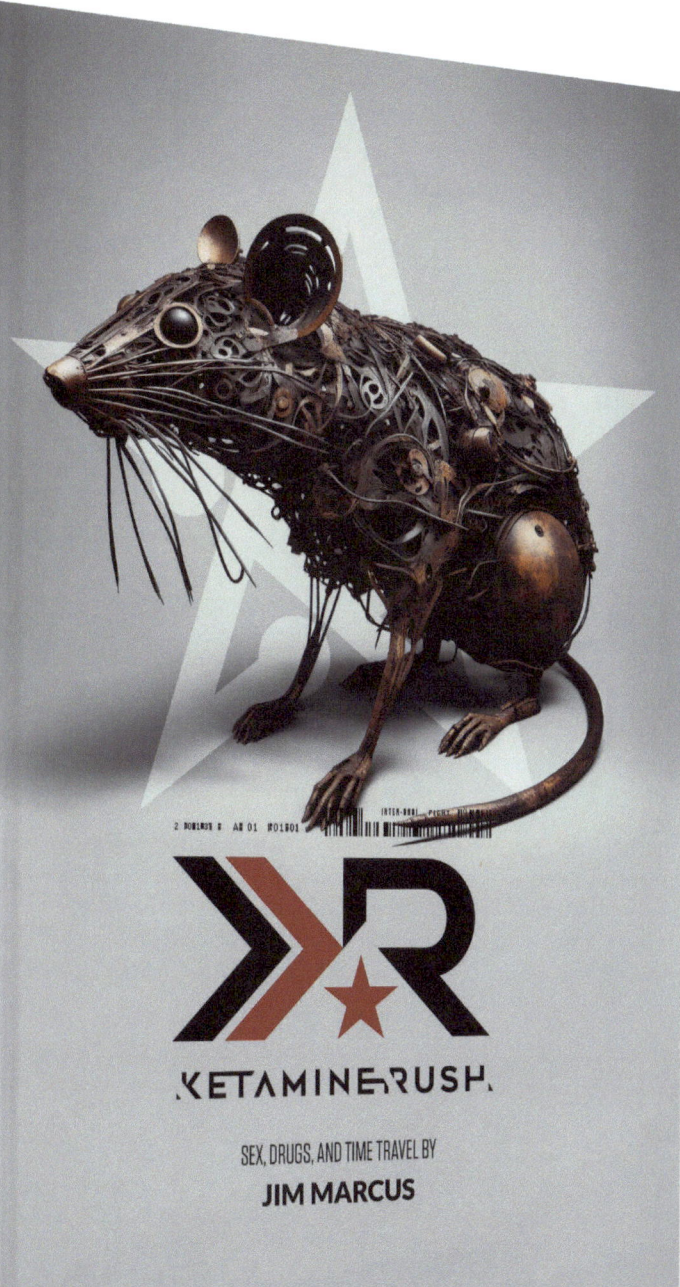

KETAMINERUSH.

SEX, DRUGS, AND TIME TRAVEL BY

JIM MARCUS

THE FUTURE OF EARTH IS ENTERTAINMENT

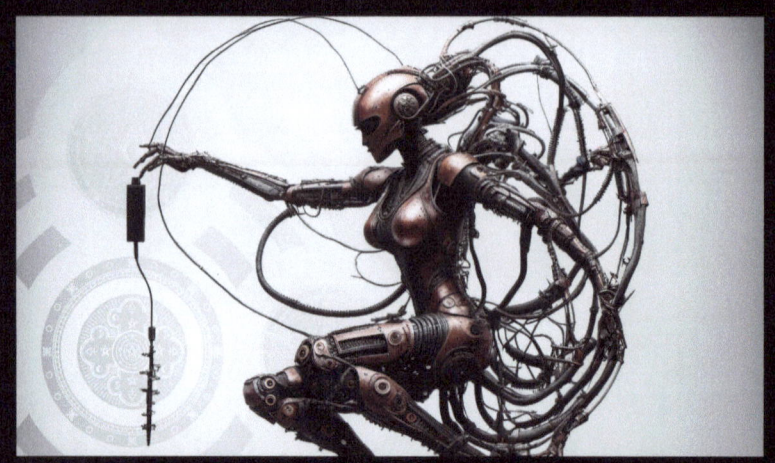

New from Go Fight and Author Jim Marcus

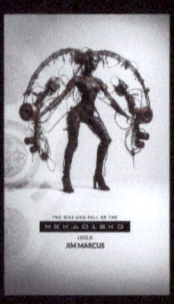

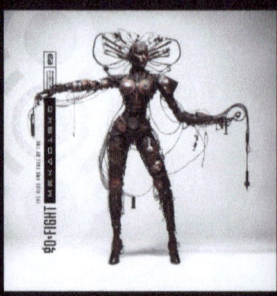

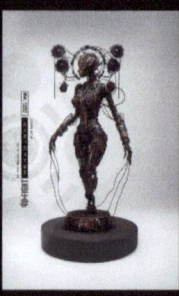

NOVEL

FULL LENGTH MUSIC CD

GRAPHIC NOVEL

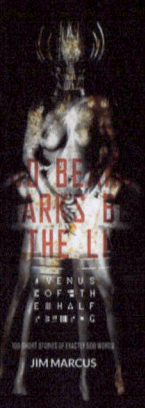

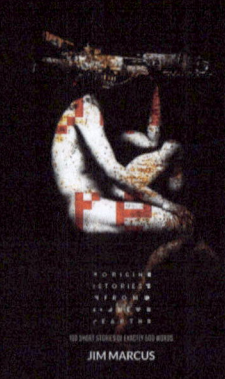

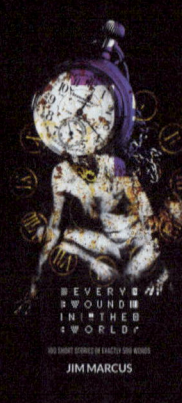

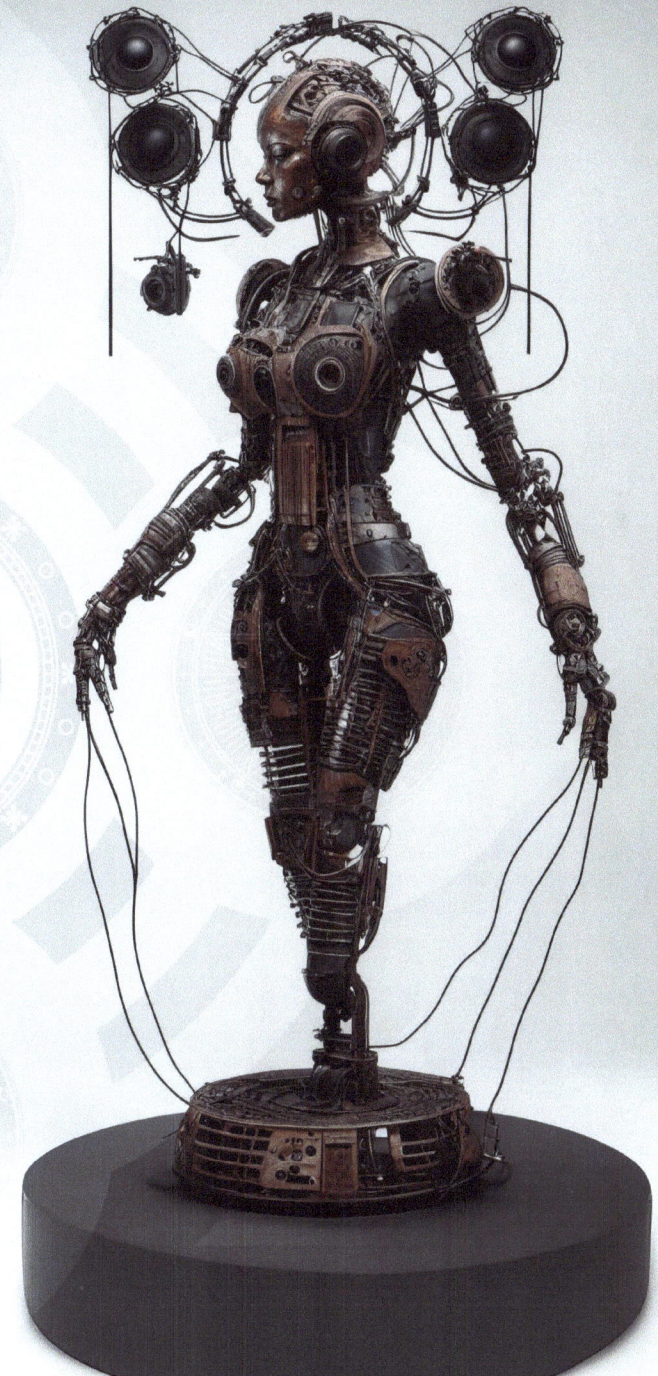

GO-"FIGHT MEKADISKO

THE RISE AND FALL OF THE

BY JIM MARCUS

43

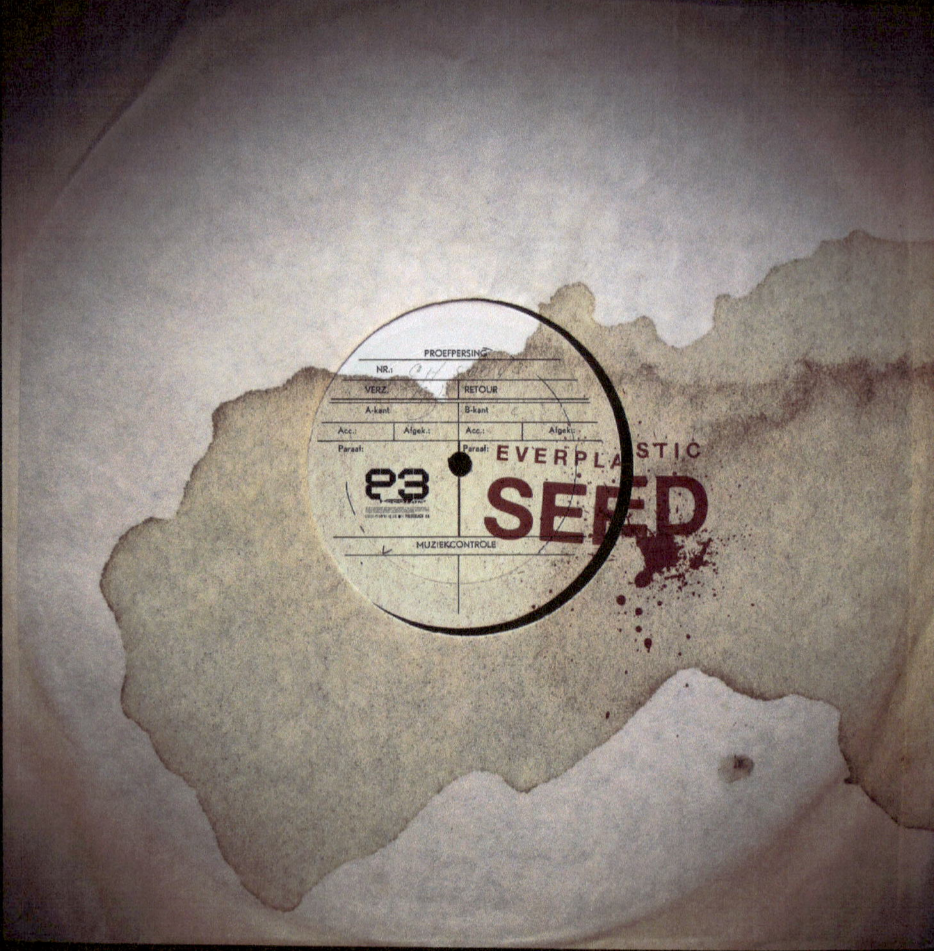

PROEFPERSING

NR.:

VERZ.   RETOUR

A-kant   B-kant

Acc.:   Afgek.:   Acc.:   Afgek.:

Paraaf: Paraaf:

EVERPLASTIC

SEED

MUZIEKCONTROLE

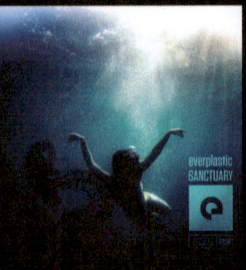

everplastic
SANCTUARY

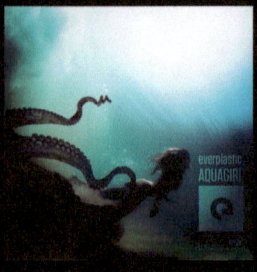

everplastic
AQUAGIRL

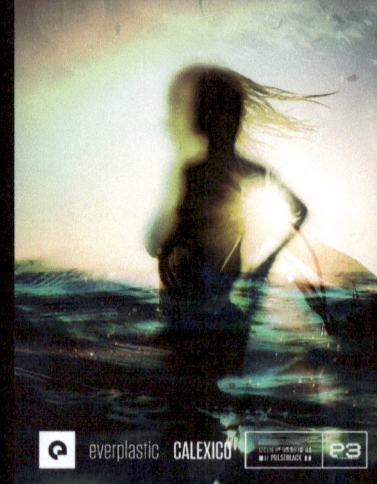

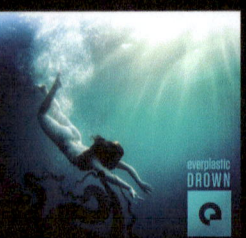

everplastic
DROWN

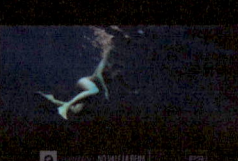

everplastic **CALEXICO**

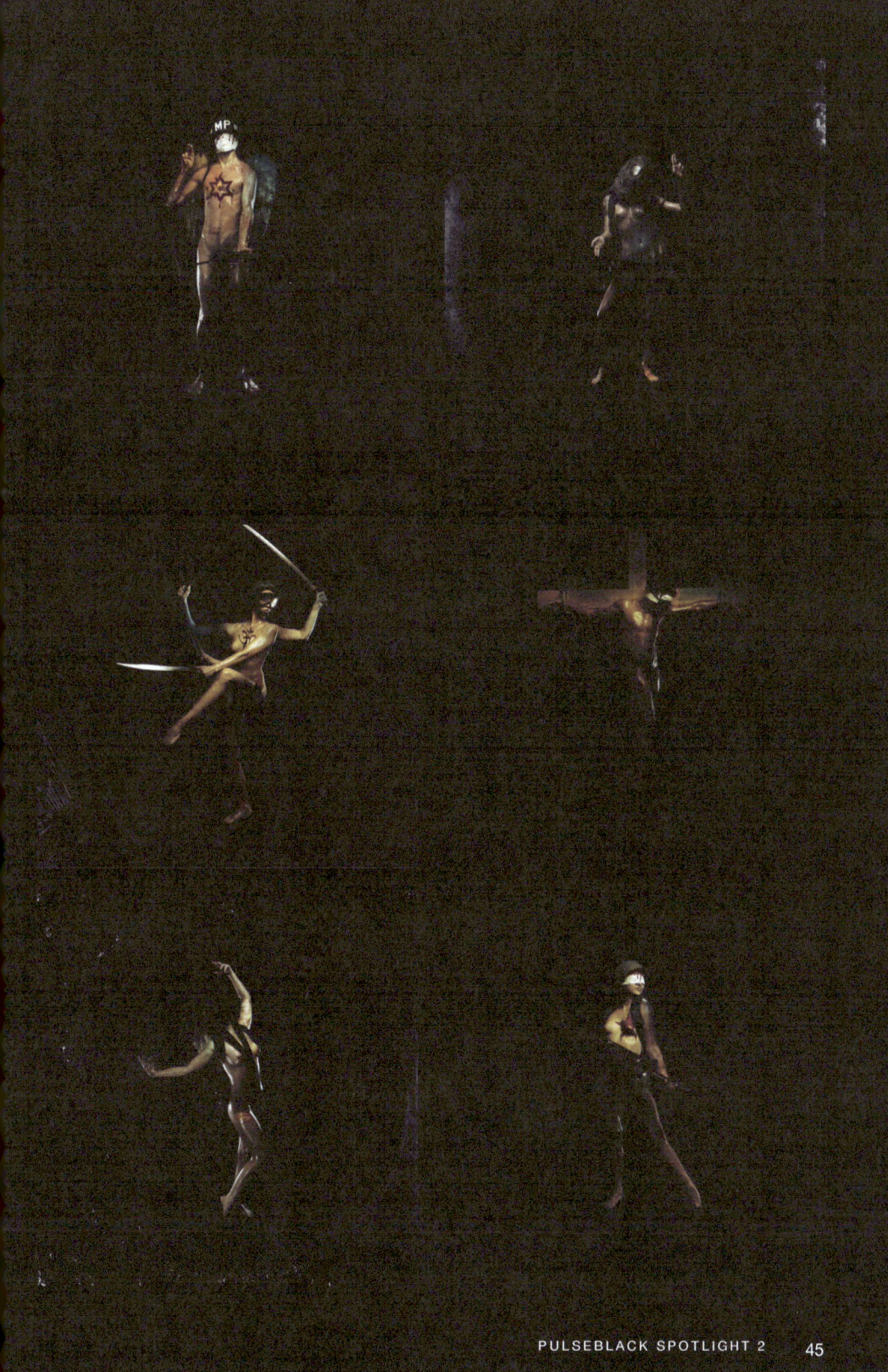

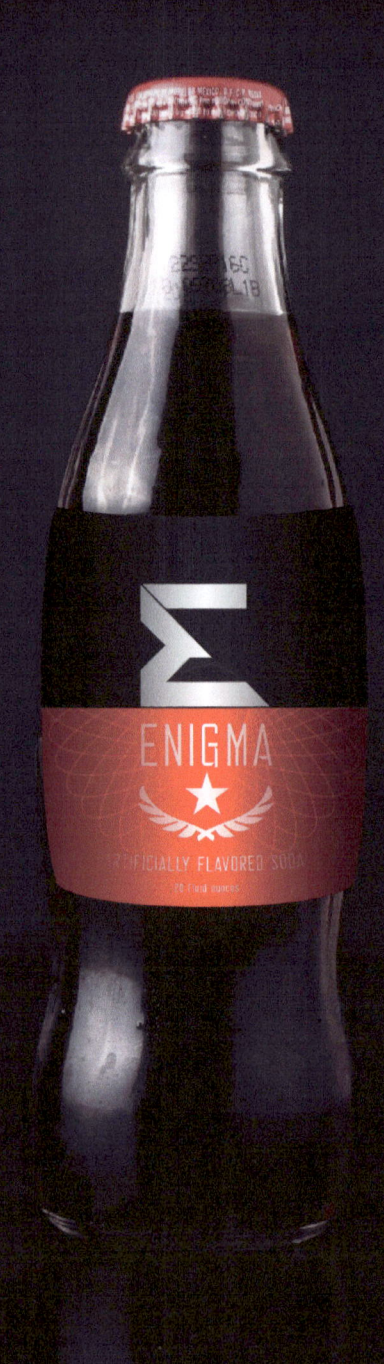

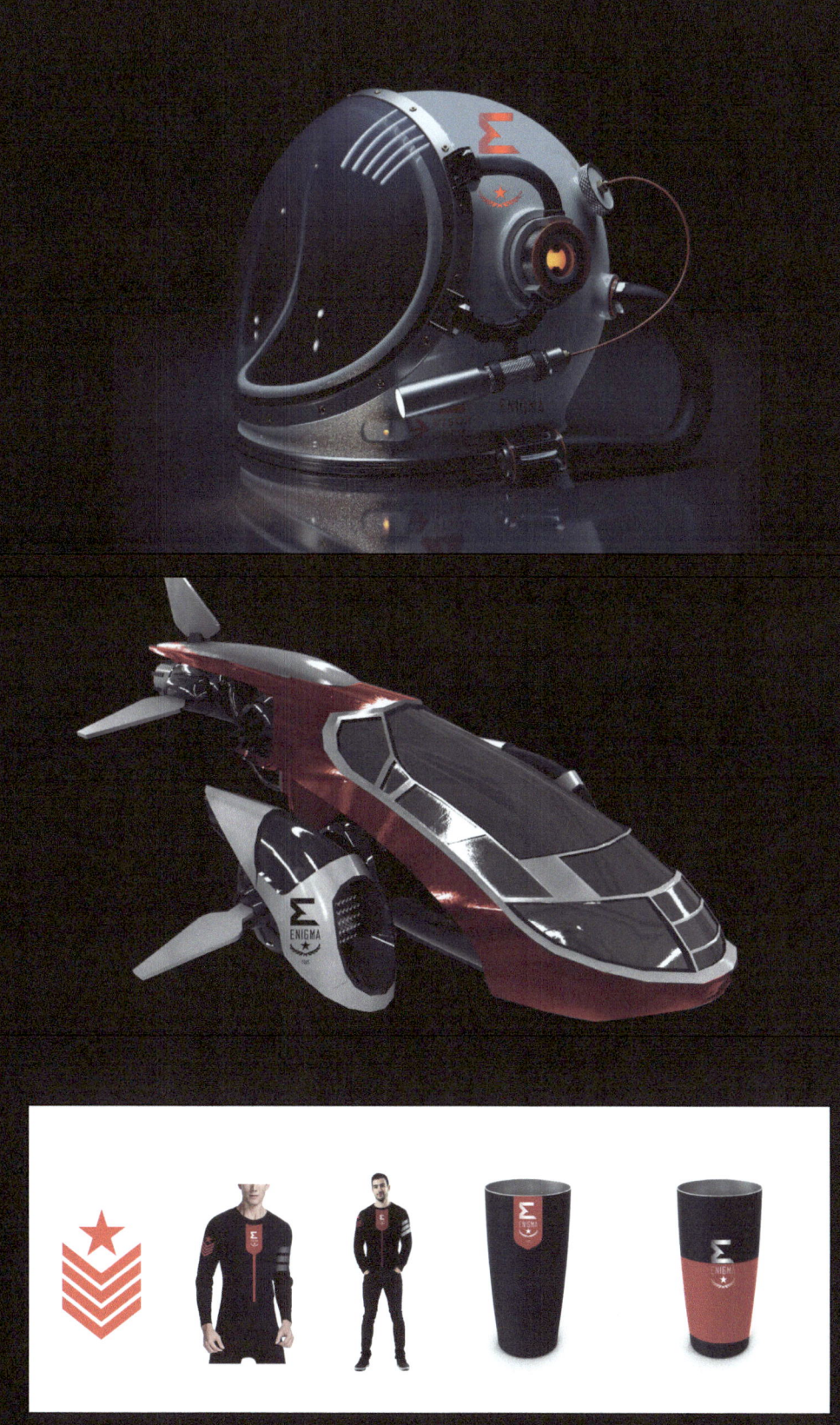

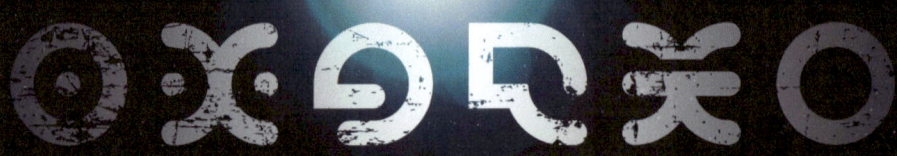

ᎤᎲᎦᏒᎲᎤ ENIGMA

ERKX1OQGS

Kateera (米ㅁ十非ㄴㅁ)

CONSONANTS

PIG	BED	TIME	DO	CHURCH	JUDGE
KILO	GO	FIVE	VERY	THINK	THE
SIX	ZOO	SHORT	CASUAL	MILK	NO
SING	HELLO	YES	READ	WINDOW	LIVE

VOWELS

SEE	SIT	BOOK	HERE	DAY
TOO	MEN	AMERICA	TOUR	BOY
WORD	SORT	CAT	GO	WEAR
BUT	PART	NOT	MY	HOW

Mirage (米非非非)

CONSONANTS

PIG	BED	TIME	DO	CHURCH	JUDGE
KILO	GO	FIVE	VERY	THINK	THE
SIX	ZOO	SHORT	CASUAL	MILK	NO
SING	HELLO	YES	READ	WINDOW	LIVE

VOWELS

SEE	SIT	BOOK	HERE	DAY
TOO	MEN	AMERICA	TOUR	BOY
WORD	SORT	CAT	GO	WEAR
BUT	PART	NOT	MY	HOW

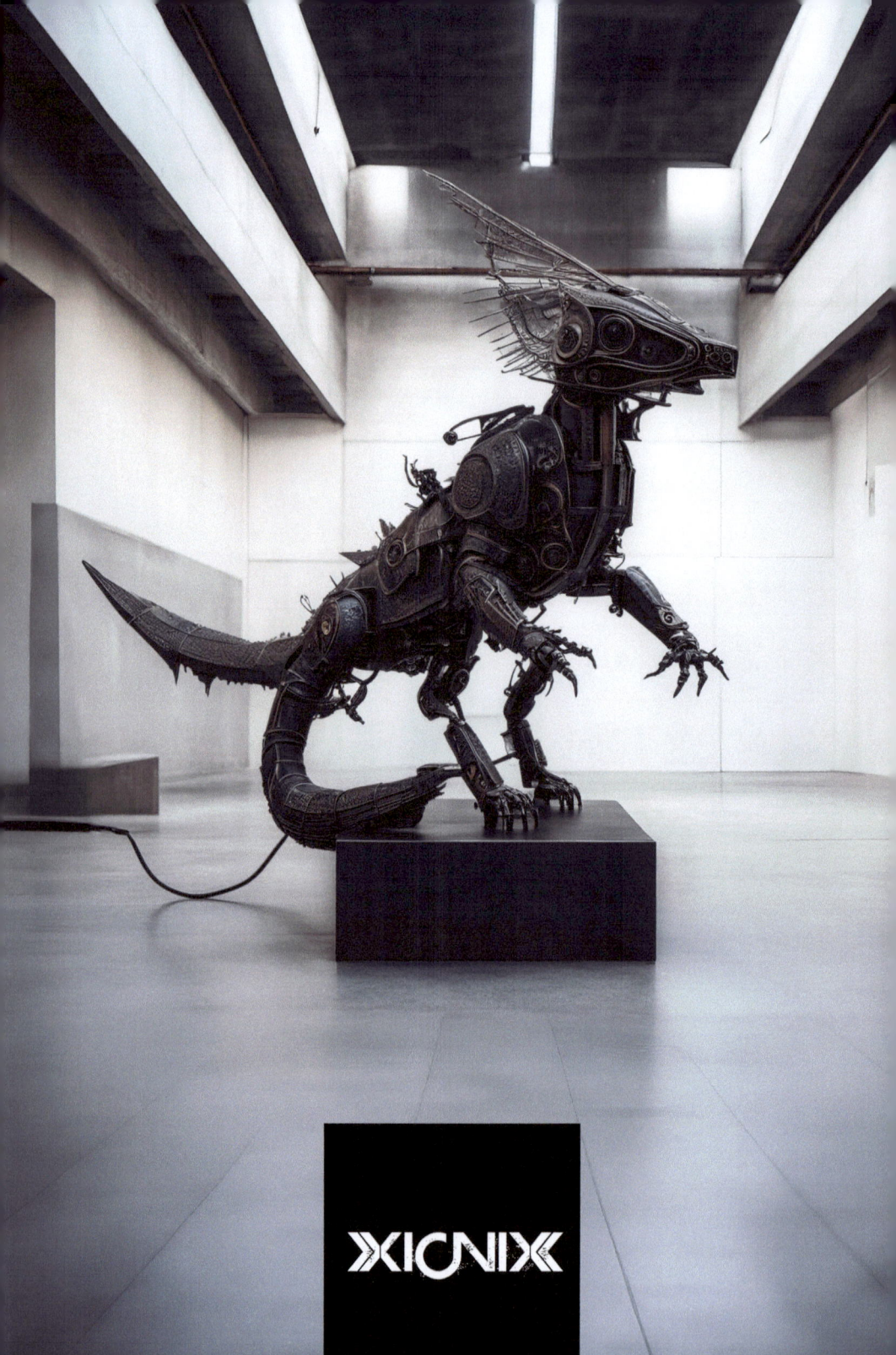

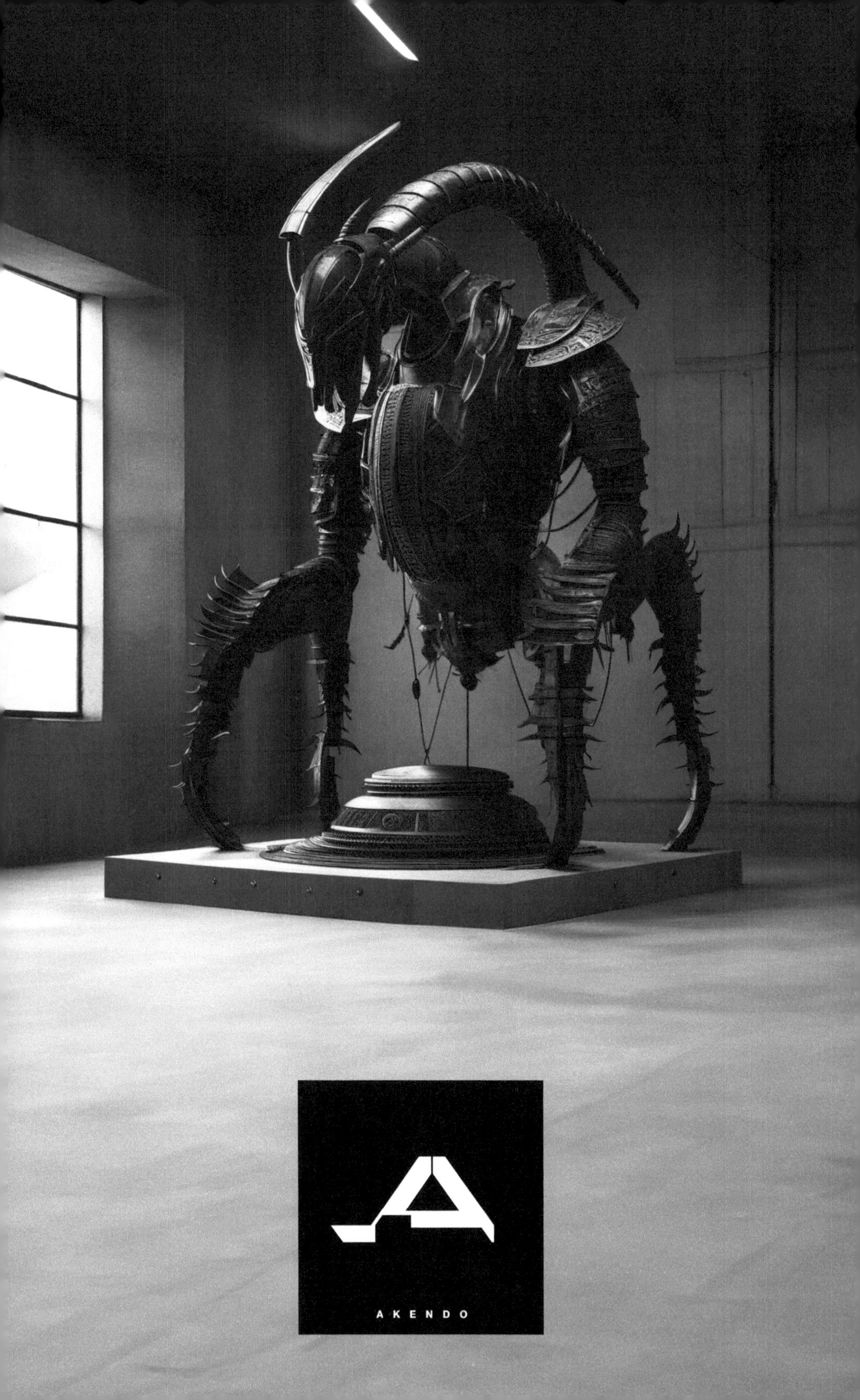

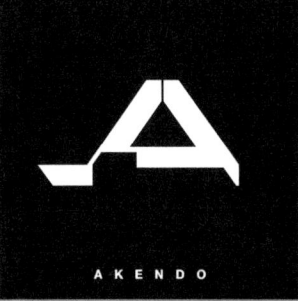

AKENDO

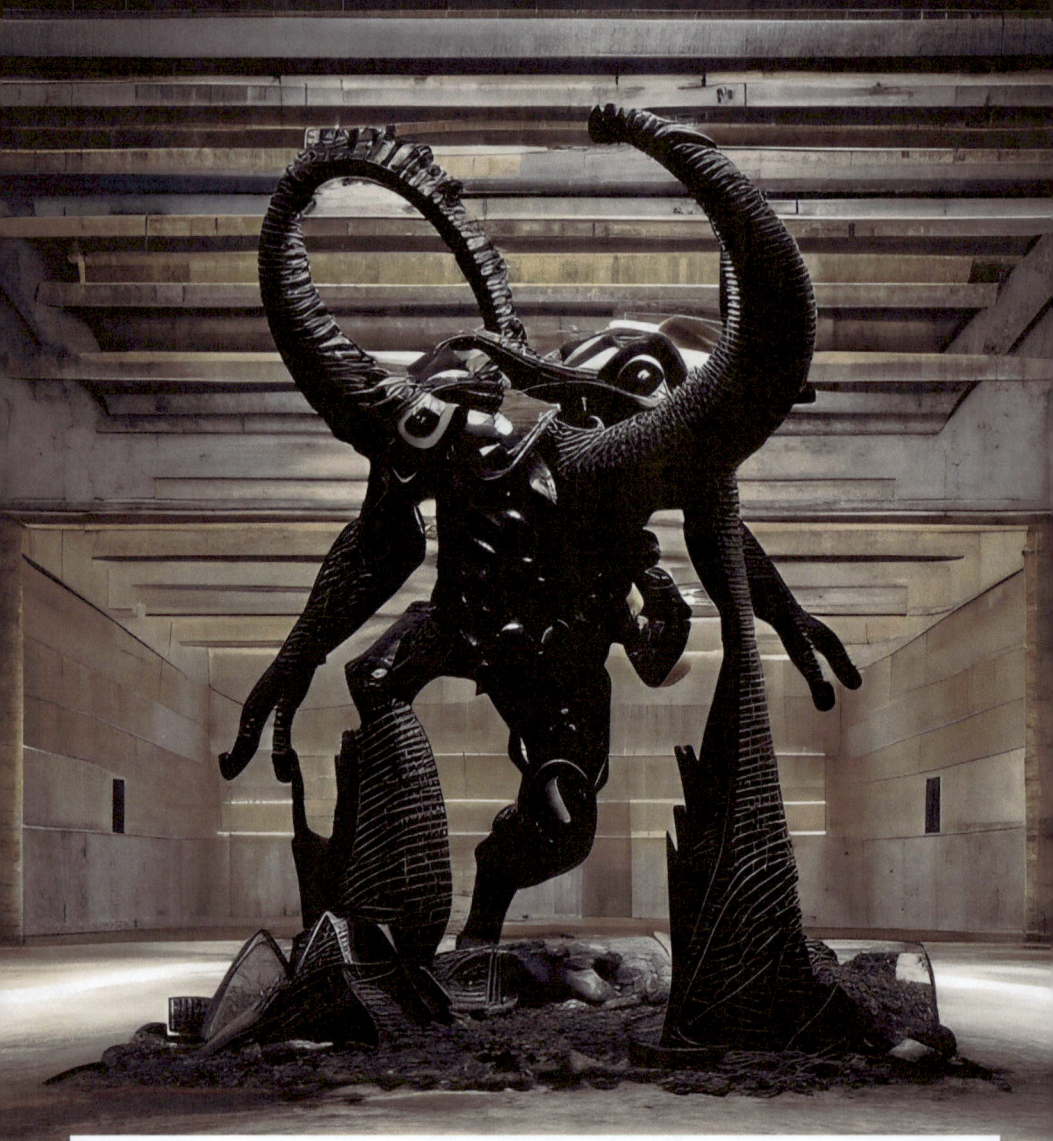

Klingon

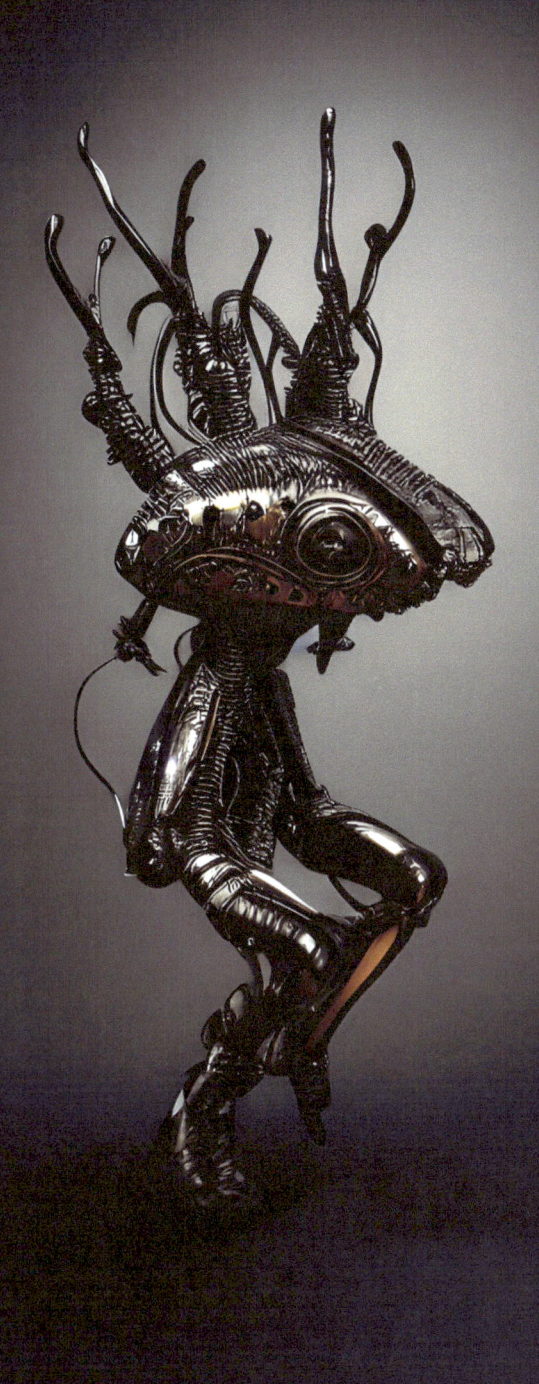

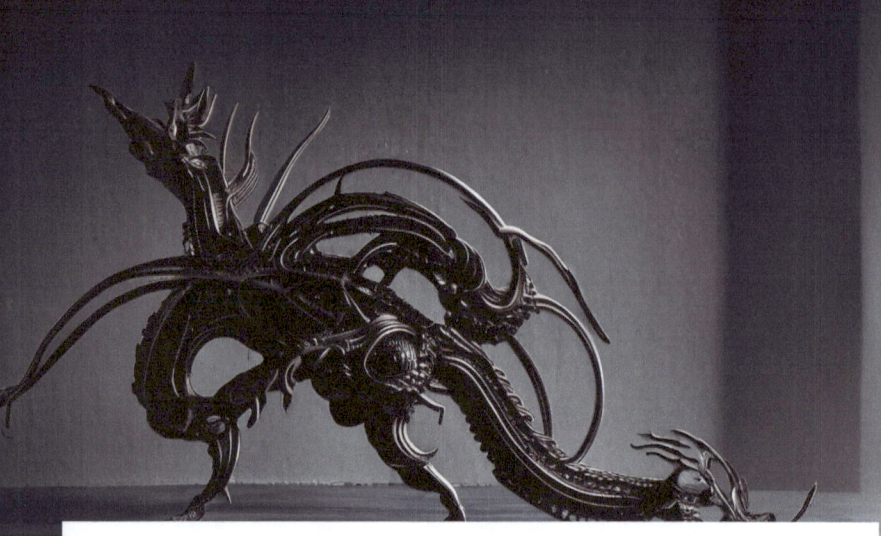

MEKADISKO

2 ░01░3░ ░   A░ 01░01░01 ░

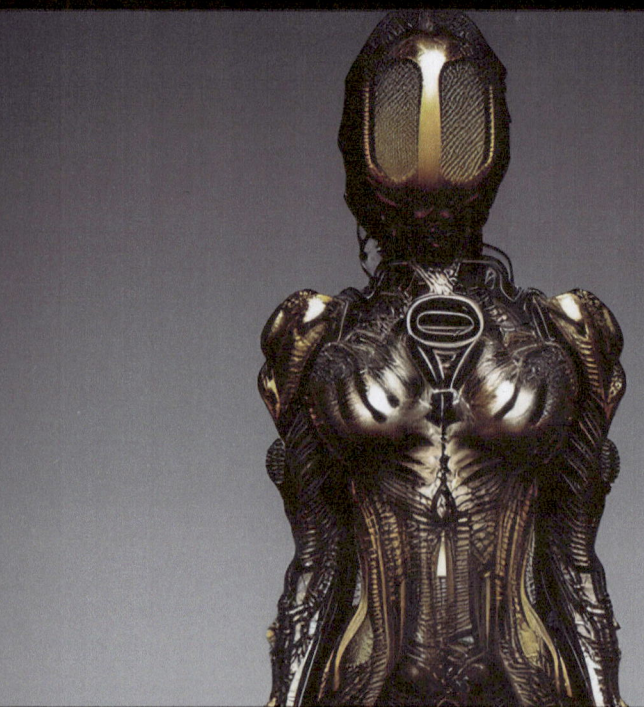

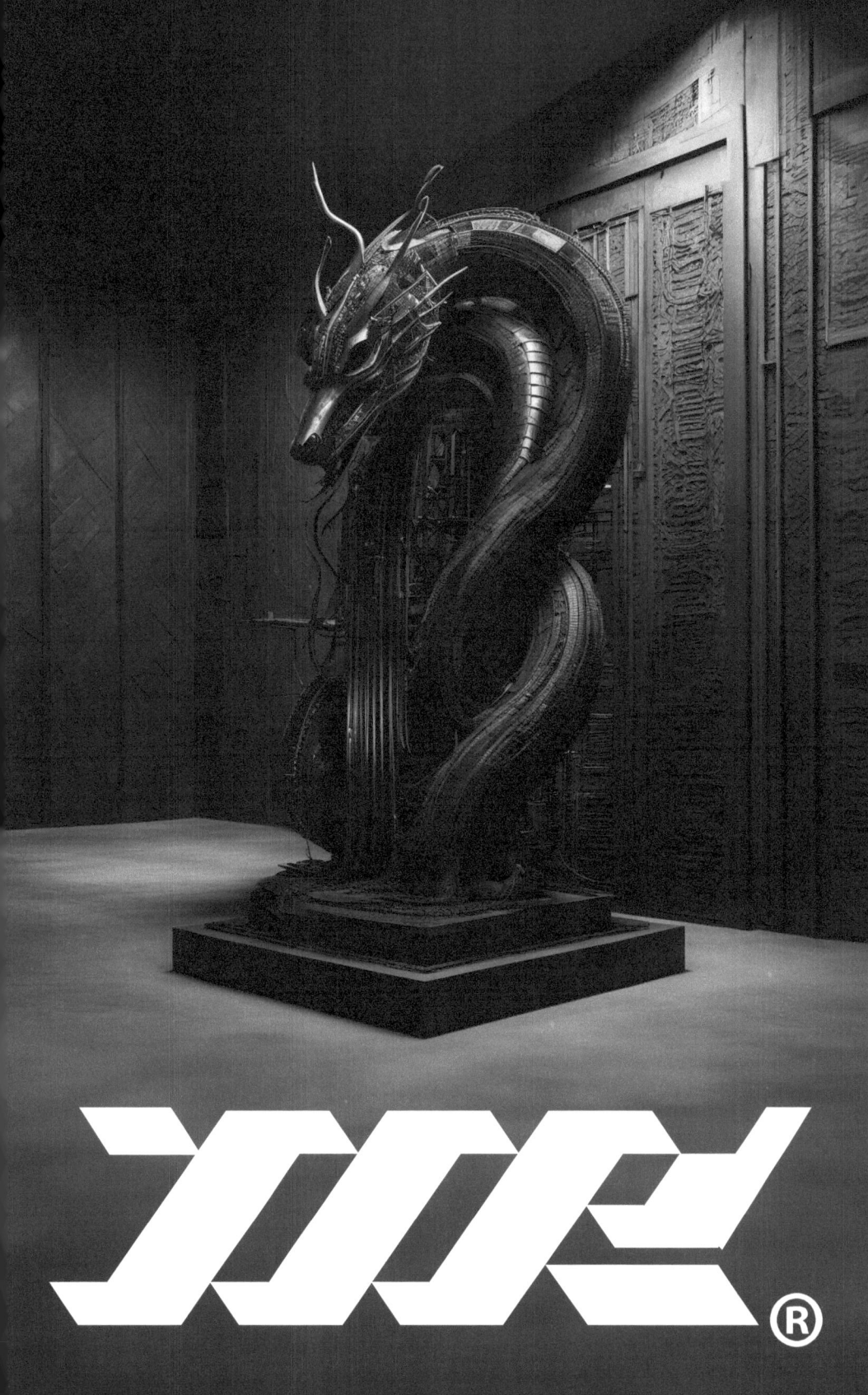

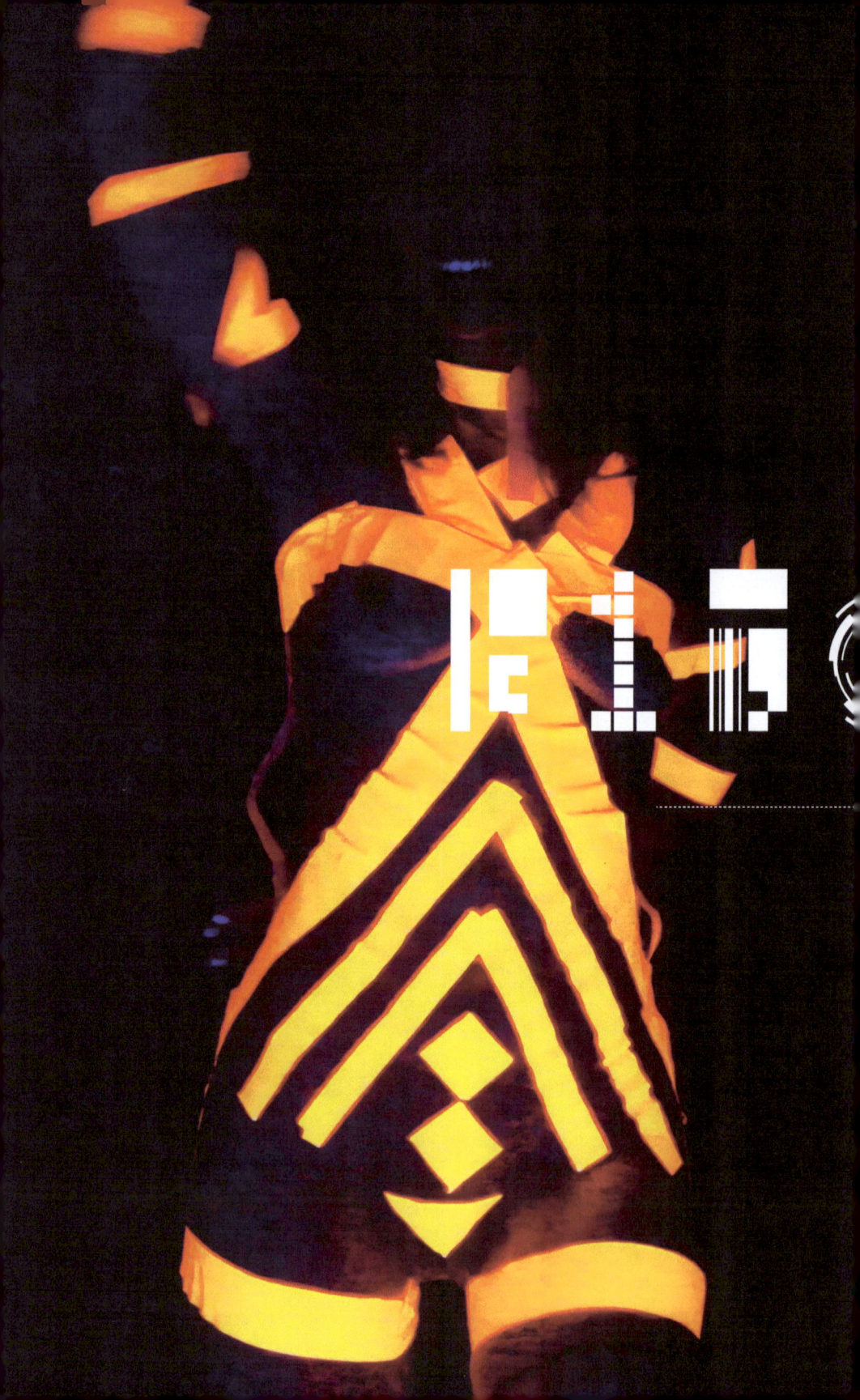

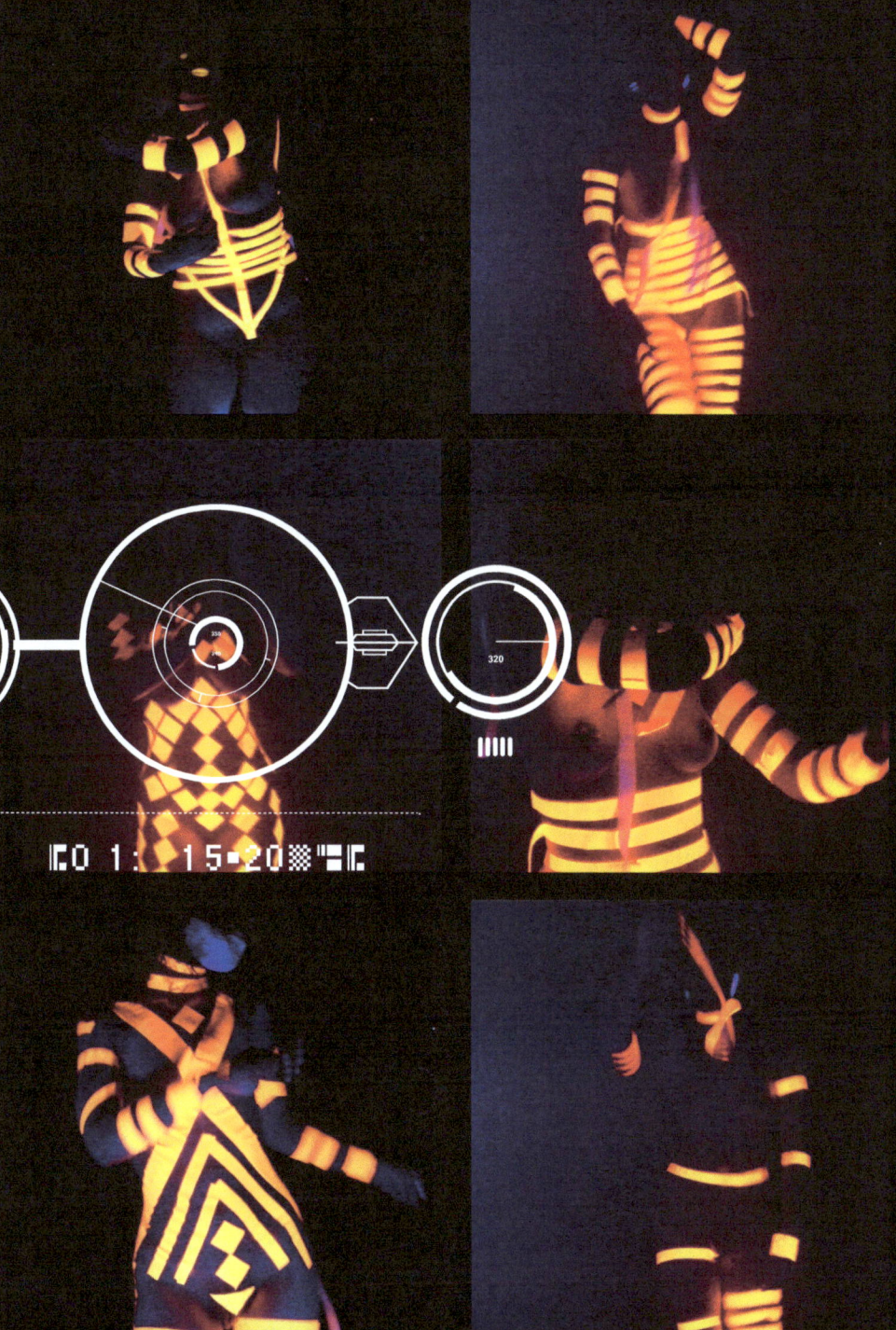

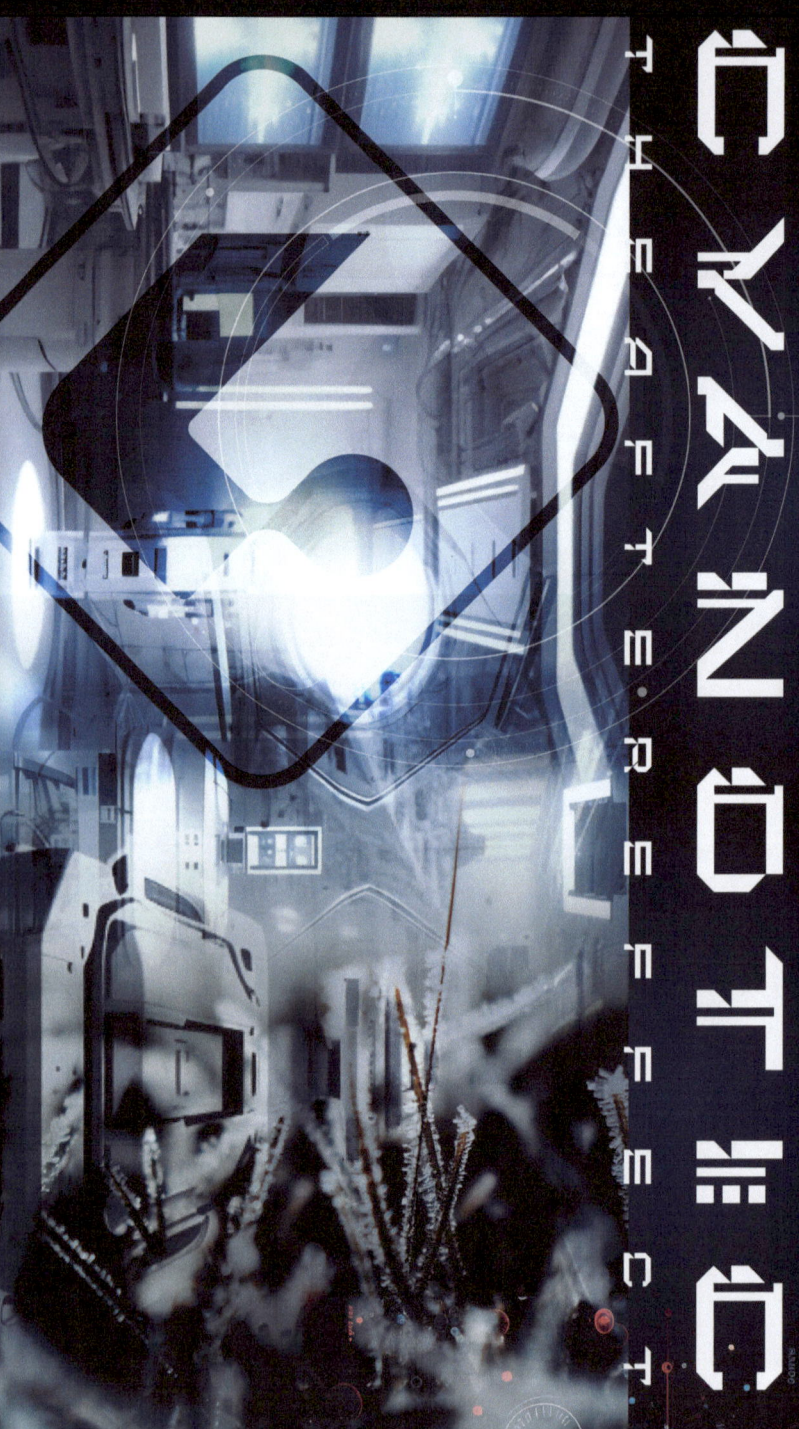

CYANOTIC

THE AFTER EFFECT

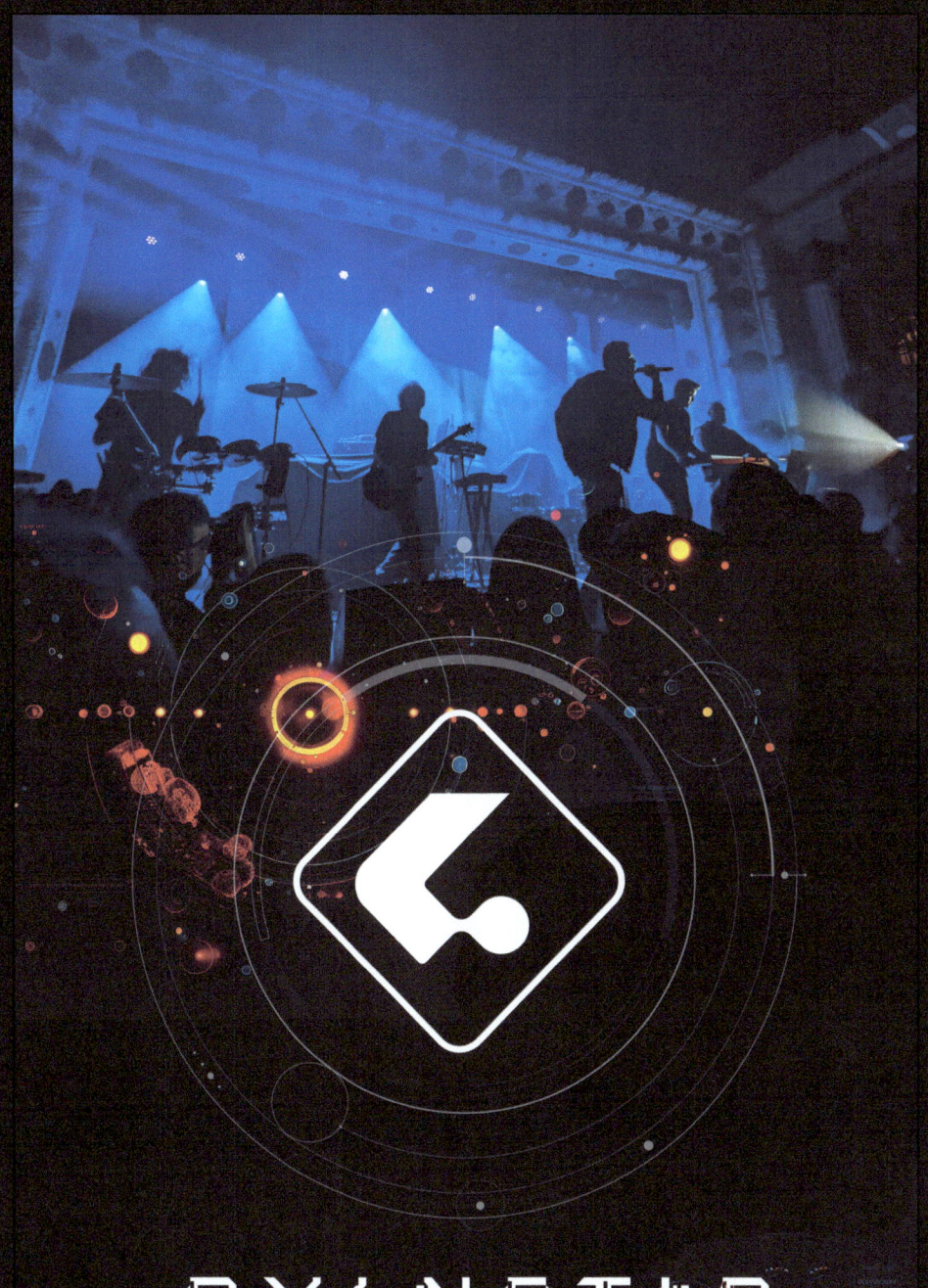

ONLINE 034 88 2RS •• LO :

CYANOTIC
THE AFTEREFFECT

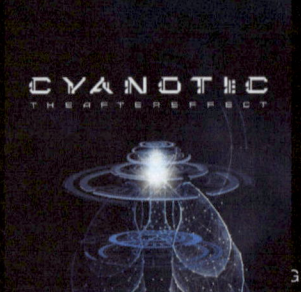

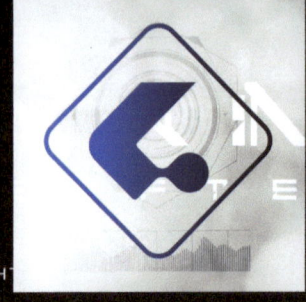

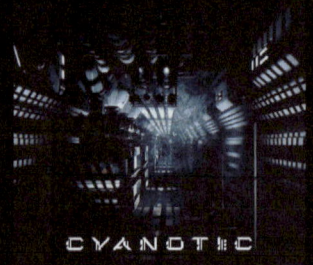

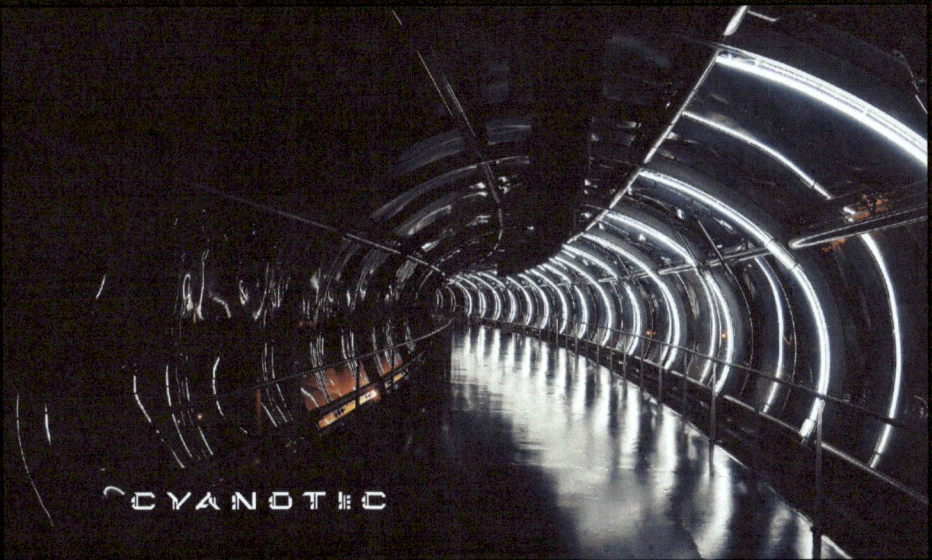

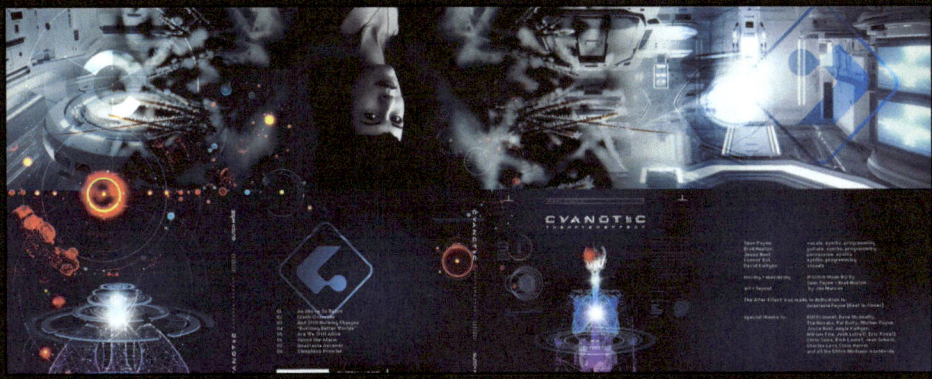

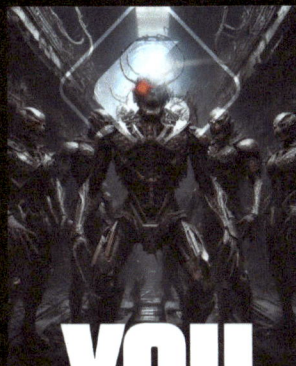
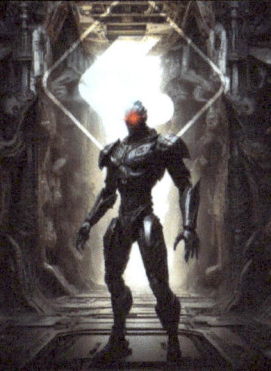
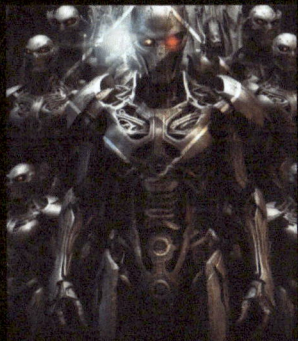

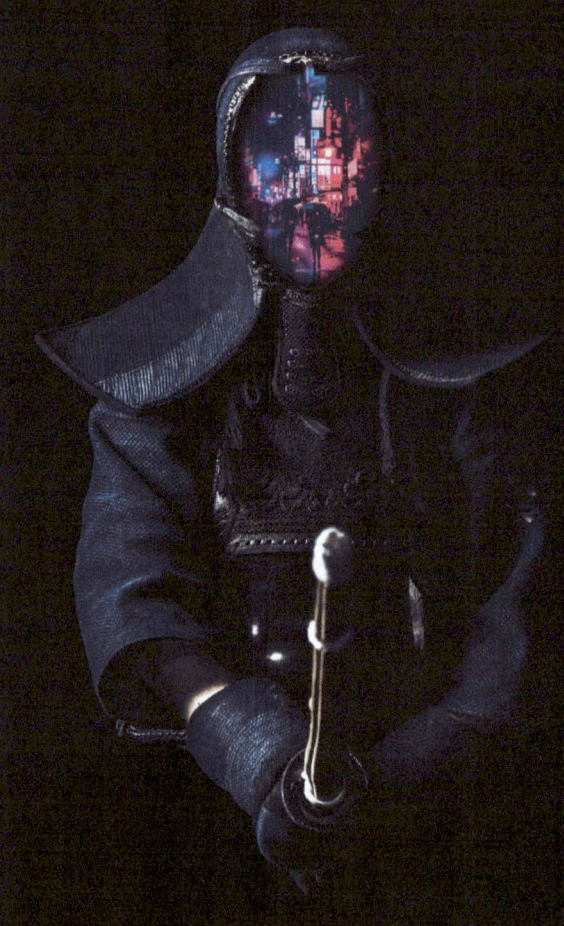

TECHNOIR

THE GLITCHMODE SHOWCASE **SATURDAY 7 | 20 | 24**

BANDS, DJS, AND MORE... GLITCH MODE RECORDINGS **MAE DISTRICT**

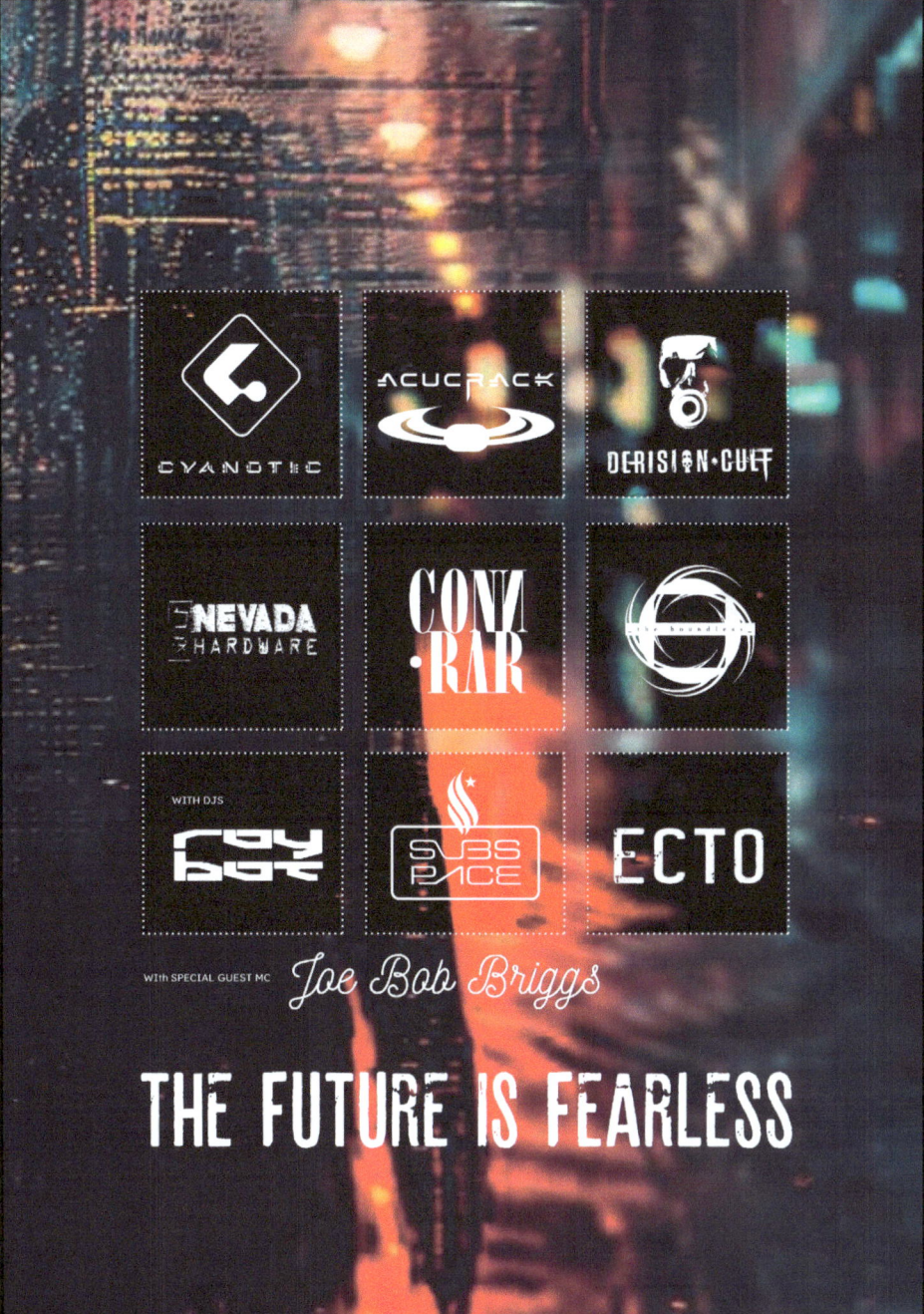

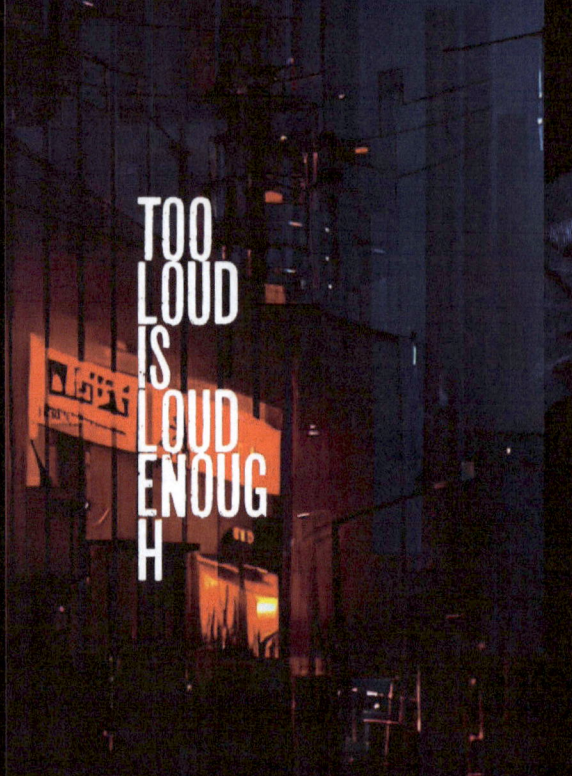

TOO LOUD IS LOUD ENOUGH

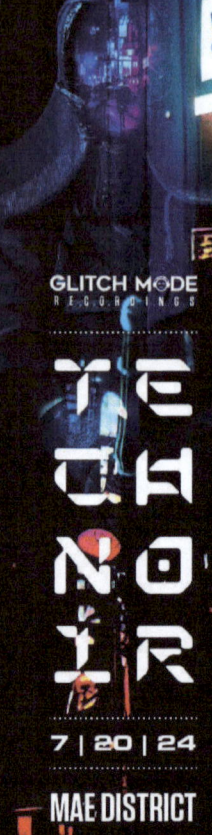

GLITCH MODE
RECORDINGS

TECHNOIR

7 | 20 | 24

MAE DISTRICT

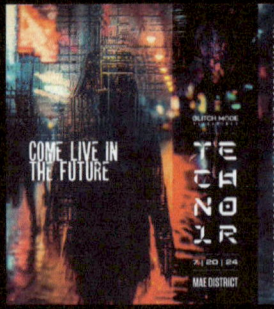

COME LIVE IN THE FUTURE

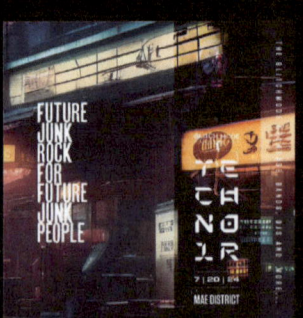

FUTURE JUNK ROCK FOR FUTURE JUNK PEOPLE

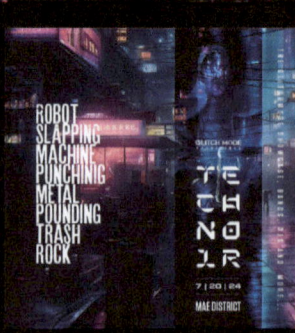

ROBOT SLAPPING MACHINE PUNCHING METAL POUNDING TRASH ROCK

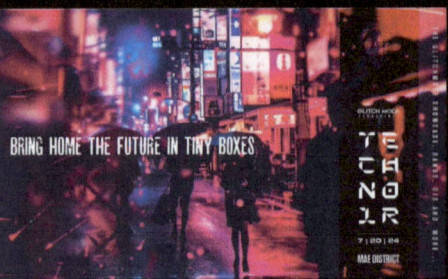

BRING HOME THE FUTURE IN TINY BOXES

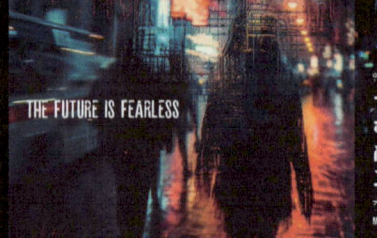

THE FUTURE IS FEARLESS

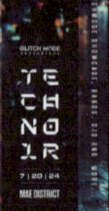

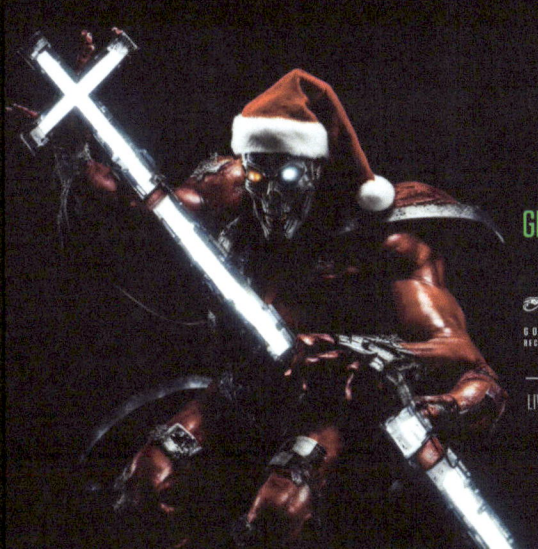

THIS YEAR, SANTA'S FUCKING KILLING IT, SO
GET ON THE FUCKING *Naughty* LIST

CLEOPATRA
GOTH / ROCK
RECORDING ARTISTS
616
AND SPECIAL GUESTS
Chicago's
DERISION·CULT
GLITCH MODE
RECORDINGS

LIVE WIRE | Thurs, DEC 14th | 8 PM | 21 and over | $10 at the door

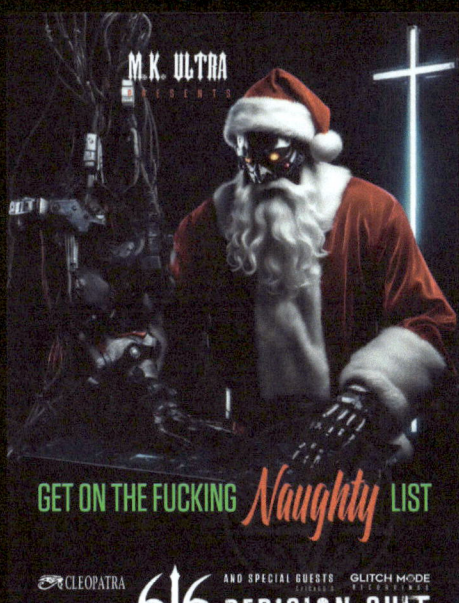

M.K. ULTRA
PRESENTS

GET ON THE FUCKING *Naughty* LIST

CLEOPATRA
GOTH / ROCK
RECORDING ARTISTS
616
AND SPECIAL GUESTS
Chicago's
DERISION·CULT
GLITCH MODE
RECORDINGS

LIVE WIRE | Thurs, DEC 14th | 8 PM | 21 and over | $10 at the door

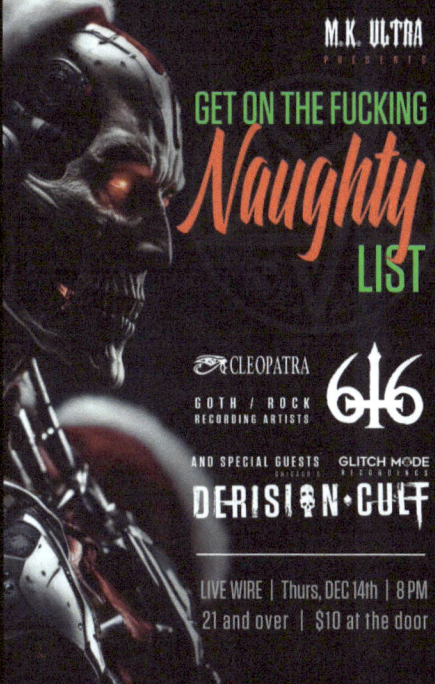

M.K. ULTRA
PRESENTS

GET ON THE FUCKING
Naughty
LIST

CLEOPATRA
GOTH / ROCK
RECORDING ARTISTS
616

AND SPECIAL GUESTS
Chicago's
DERISION·CULT
GLITCH MODE
RECORDINGS

LIVE WIRE | Thurs, DEC 14th | 8 PM
21 and over | $10 at the door

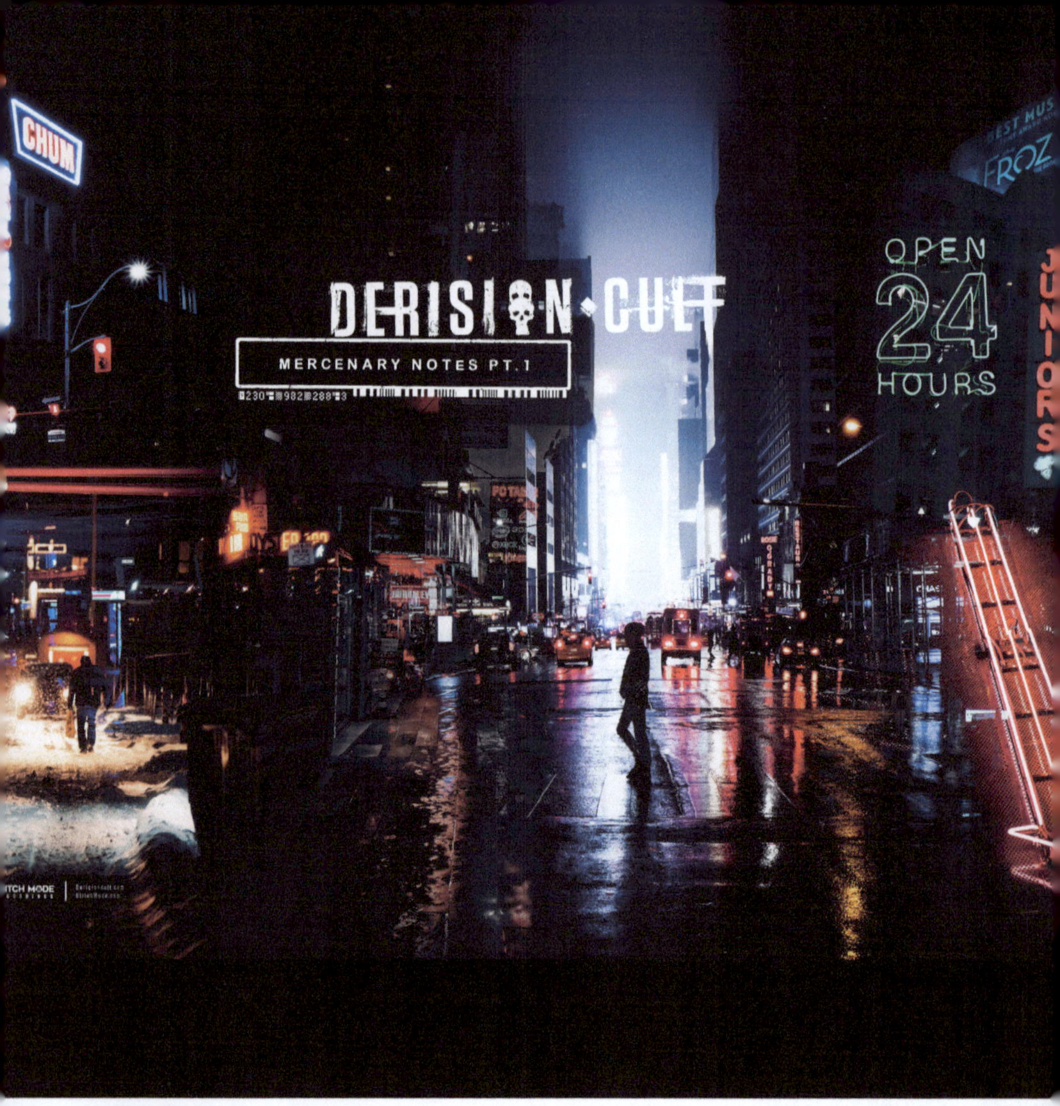

DERISION·CULT

MERCENARY NOTES PT. 1

230▪▪▪982▪288▪3

DERISION·CULT

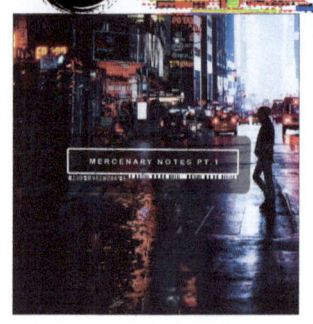

MERCENARY NOTES PT 1

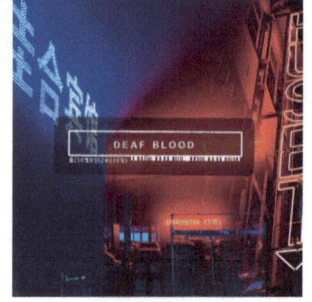

DEAF BLOOD

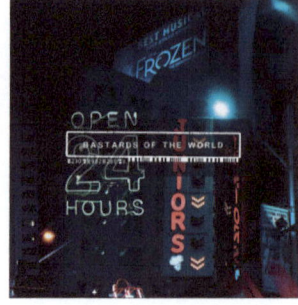

BASTARDS OF THE WORLD

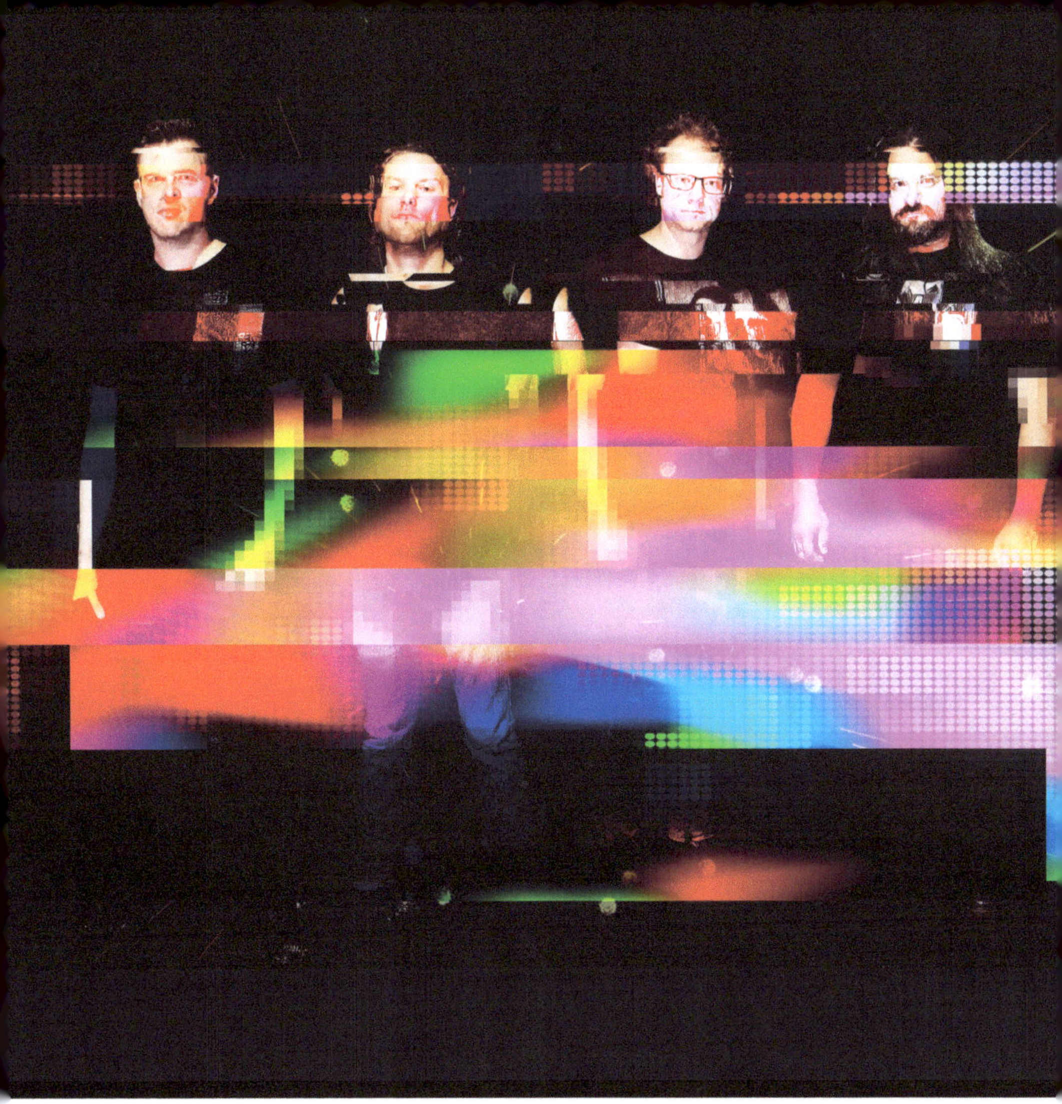

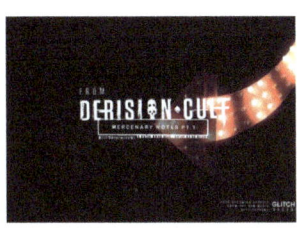
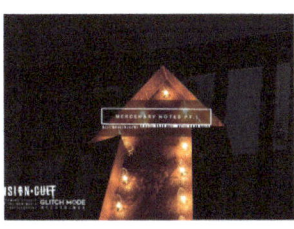
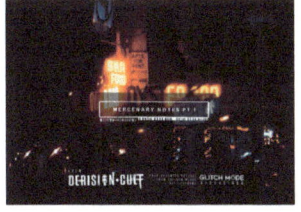
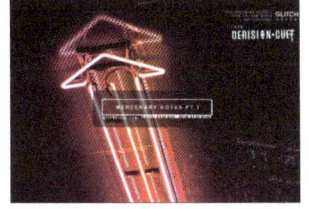
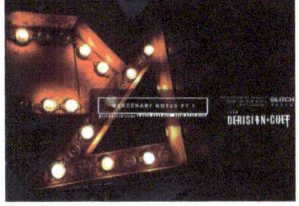
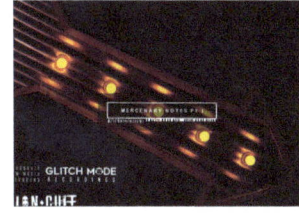

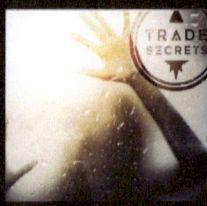

TRADESECRETS
BEFORE WE VANISH
消え去る前に

1 ANSWERS
2 BROKEN INSTINCTS
3 TRUE NORTH
4 YOUR HEAVEN (Before We Vanish)
5 ULTRA DEVIL
6 REFACTORED
7 GAMES
8 WISH FOR THE REST
9 TOO MANY TOMORROWS

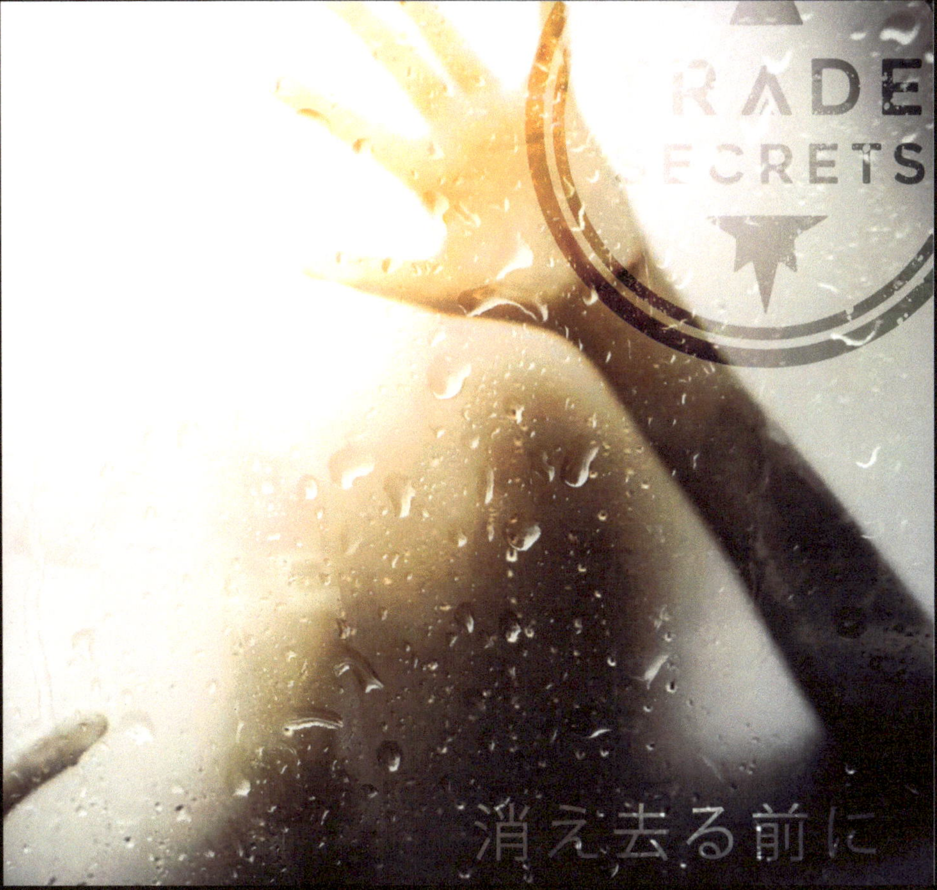

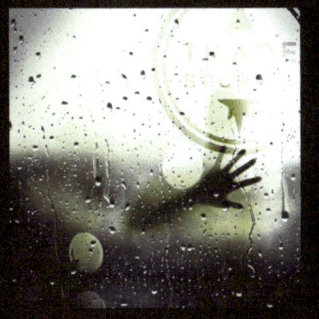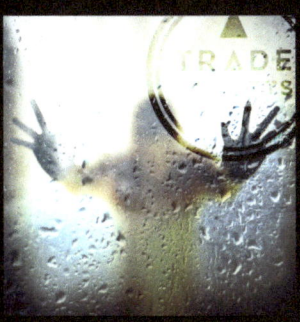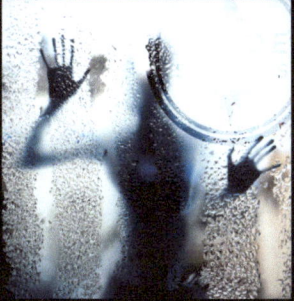
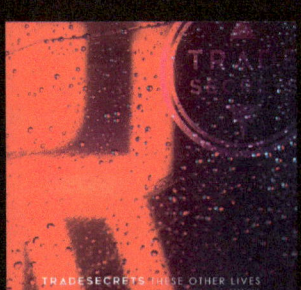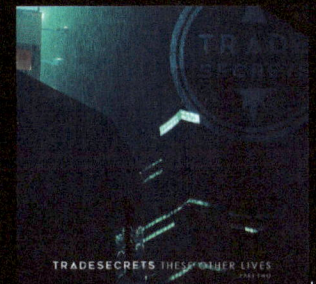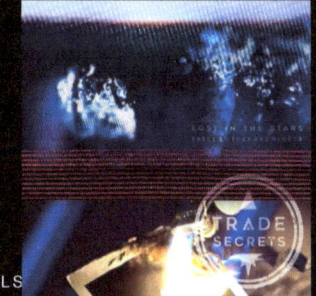

7 ASPECTS | 3 LEVELS

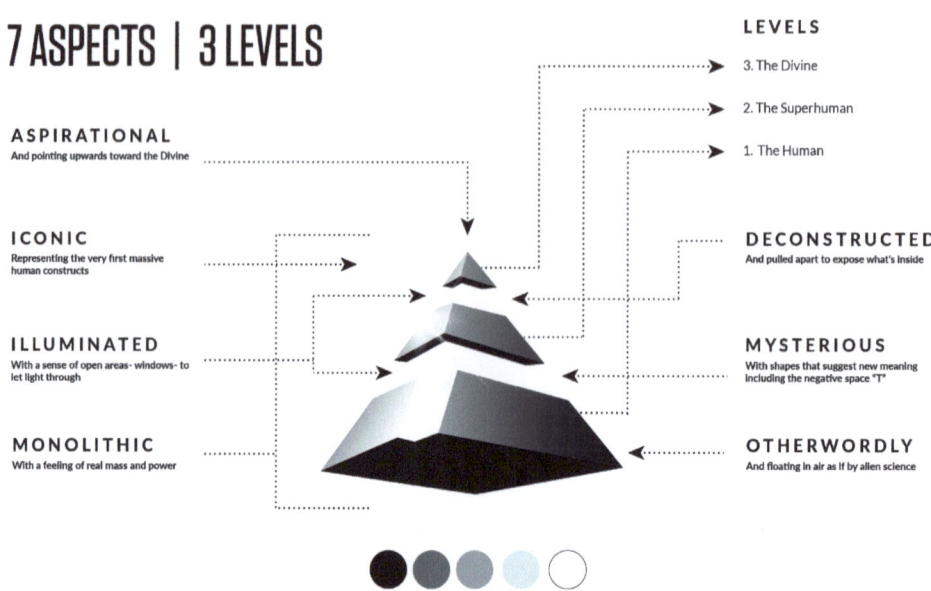

LEVELS

3. The Divine

2. The Superhuman

1. The Human

ASPIRATIONAL
And pointing upwards toward the Divine

ICONIC
Representing the very first massive human constructs

ILLUMINATED
With a sense of open areas- windows- to let light through

MONOLITHIC
With a feeling of real mass and power

DECONSTRUCTED
And pulled apart to expose what's inside

MYSTERIOUS
With shapes that suggest new meaning including the negative space "T"

OTHERWORDLY
And floating in air as if by alien science

ALIENESQUE
With shapes like this "A"

POWERFUL
LOW CENTER OF GRAVITY AND THICK

SIMPLE
AND ELEGANT

MODERN
LEGIBLE QUICKLY AND WITHOUT ARTIFICE

TRANSFIX
A TRAVELING GALLERY OF HUMAN MAGNITUDE

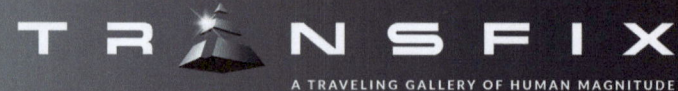

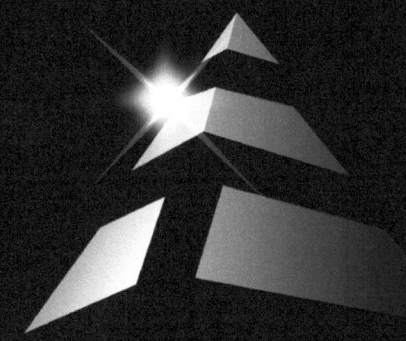

T R A N S F I X

A TRAVELING GALLERY OF HUMAN MAGNITUDE

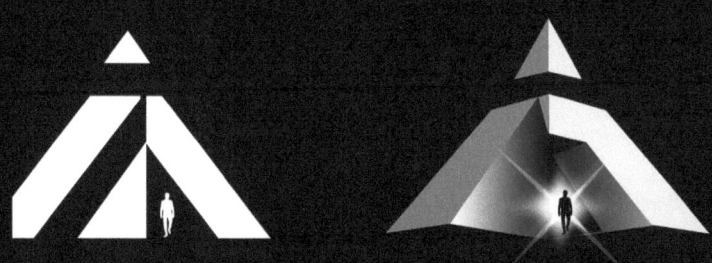

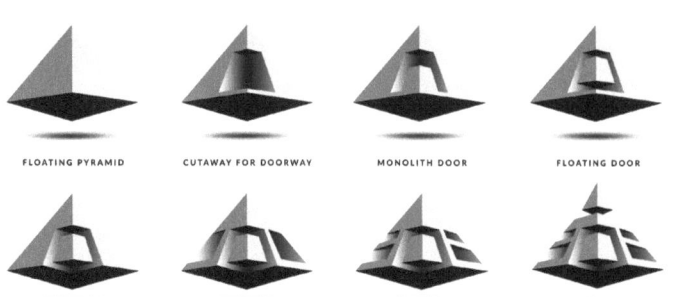

| FLOATING PYRAMID | CUTAWAY FOR DOORWAY | MONOLITH DOOR | FLOATING DOOR |

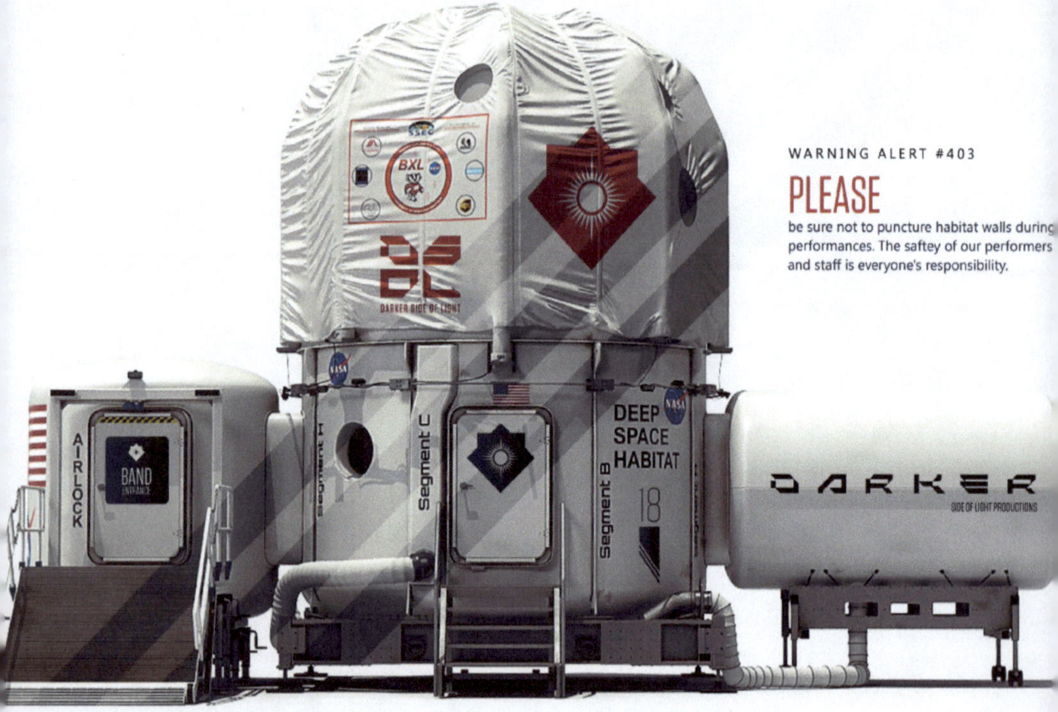

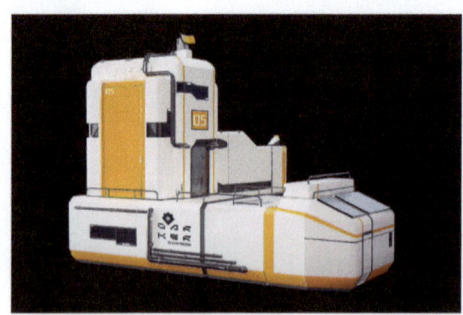

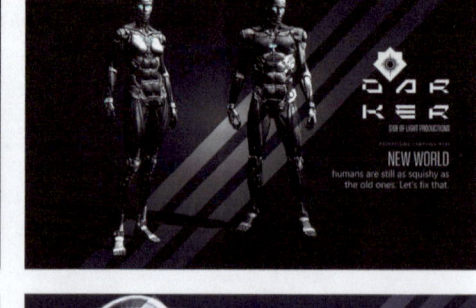

NEW WORLD
humans are still as squishy as the old ones. Let's fix that.

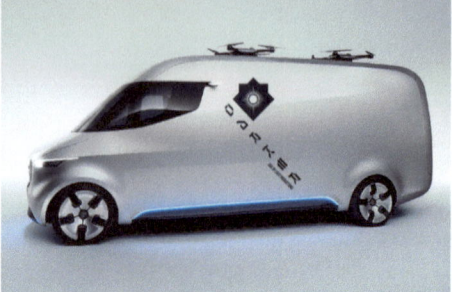

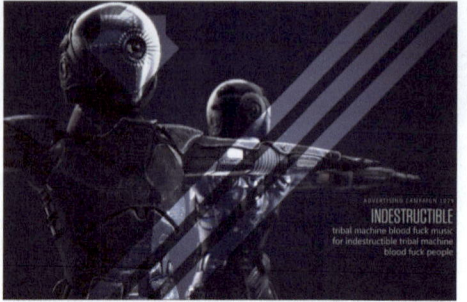

INDESTRUCTIBLE
tribal machine blood fuck music for indestructible tribal machine blood fuck people

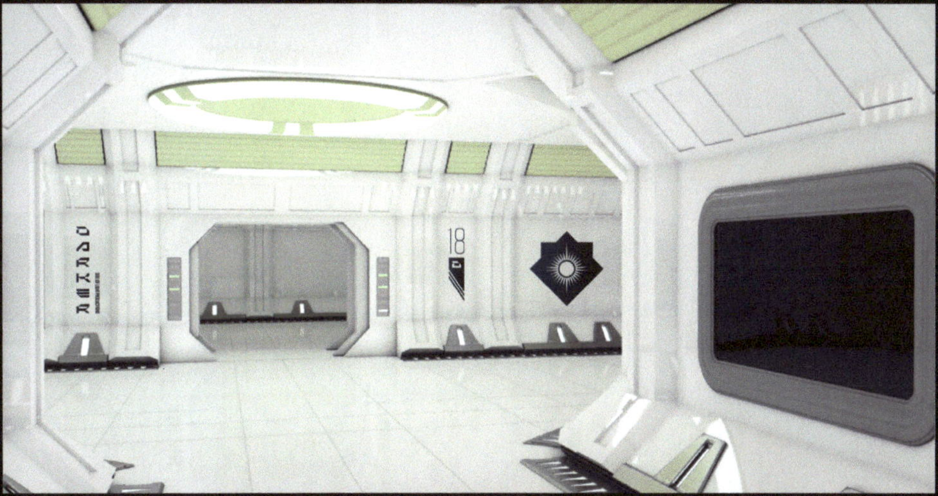

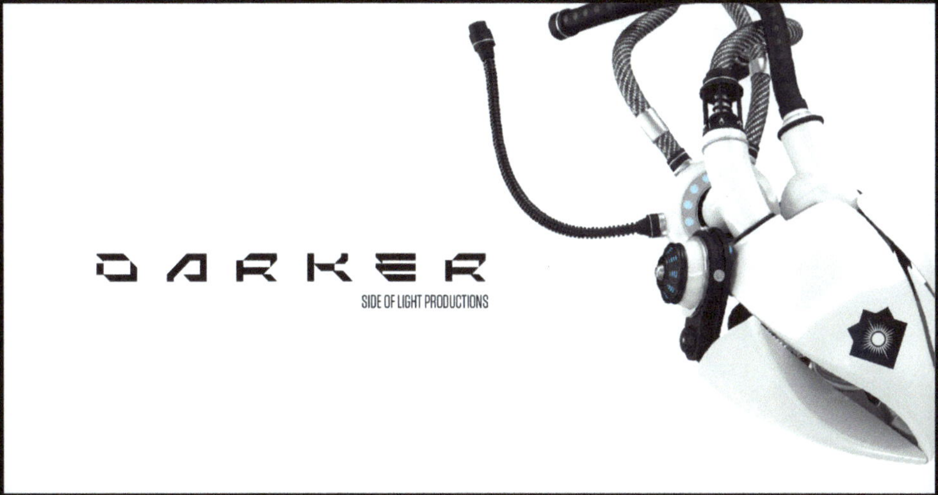

DARKER
SIDE OF LIGHT PRODUCTIONS

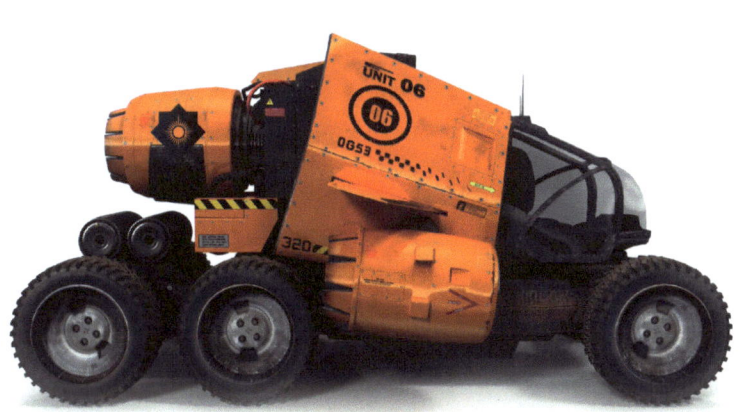

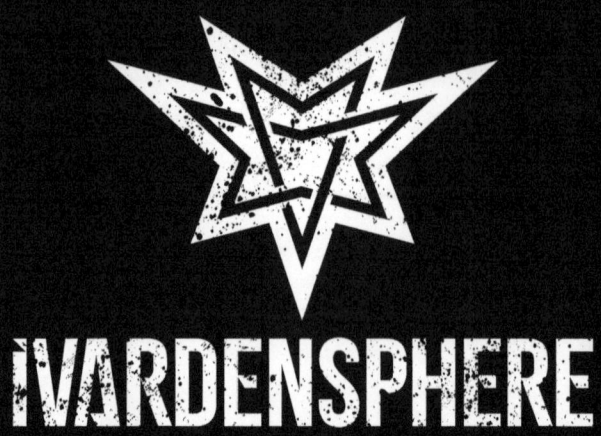

IVARDENSPHERE

EVERFEAR

A B C D E F G H I J K LL M

N O P Q R S TT U V W X Y Z

1 2 3 4 5 6 7 8 9 0

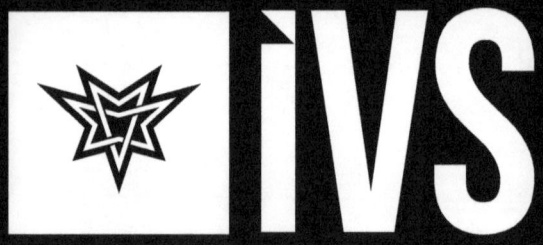

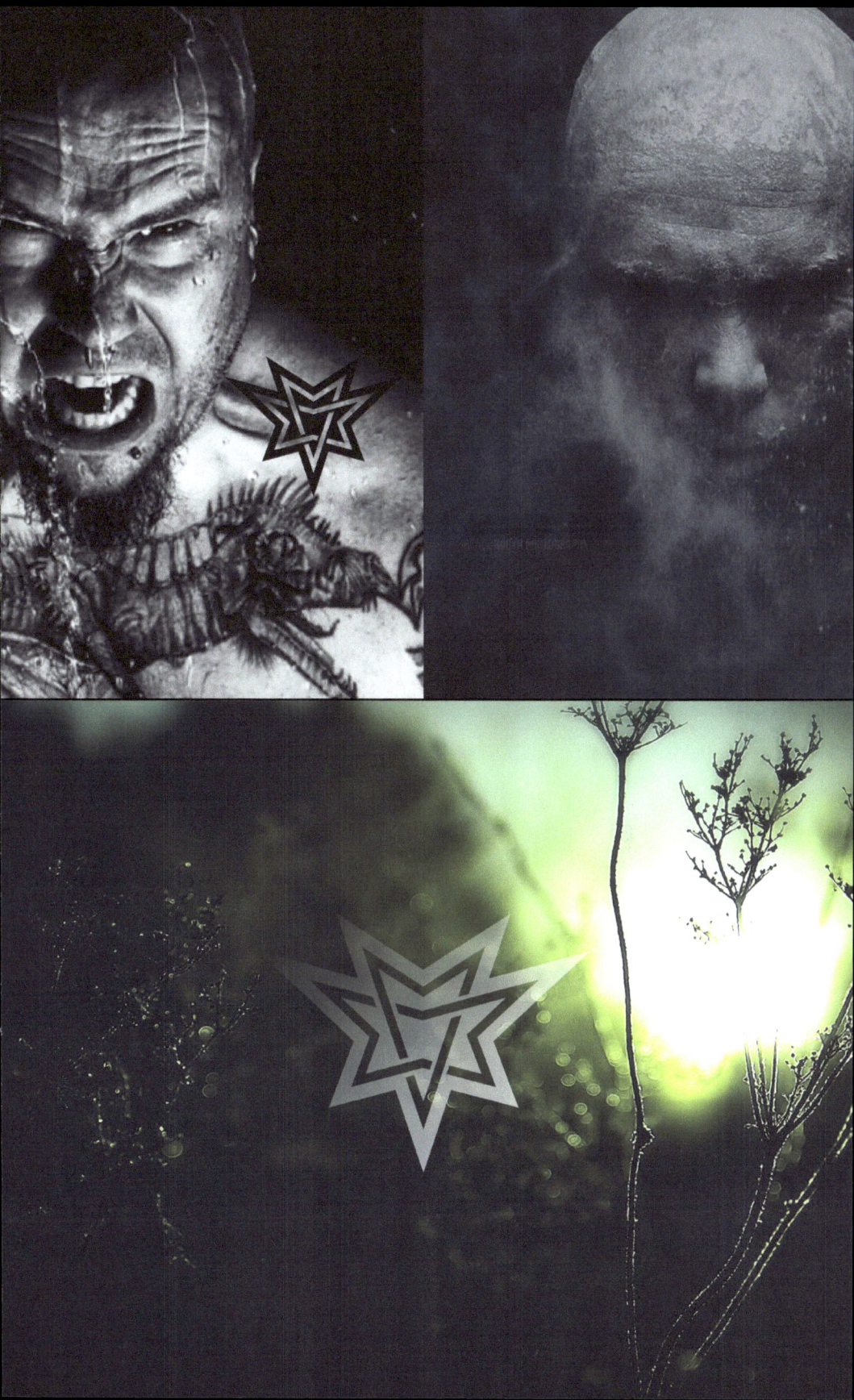

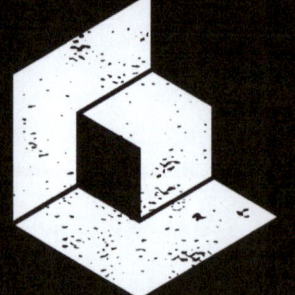

CUBANATE
BRUTAL1SM

Acceptable Executions

Standard elements

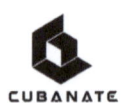

The logo as it is expressed normally

Separated

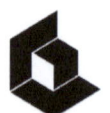

The 2 different pieces don't always need to be used together.

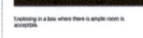

The 2 different pieces don't always need to be used together.

Enclosed

Enclosing in a box where there is ample room is acceptable.

Enclosing in a box where there is ample room is acceptable.

Distressed

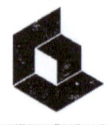

It is acceptable to merge with or render as grunge.

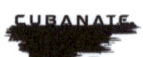

It is acceptable to merge with or render as grunge.

Partially Enclosed

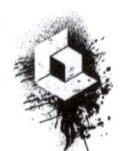

Partially enclosing the pieces in grunge elements is acceptable.

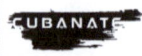

Partially enclosing the pieces in grunge elements is acceptable.

Overprinted

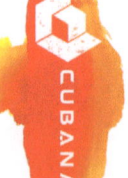

Overprinting in the base color over a shape is acceptable.

Horizontal

Century Gothic is used across the collateral. Bold is only used at small sizes or for a few numbers or letters at larger sizes.

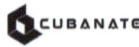

Ghosted

Century Gothic is used across the collateral. Bold is only used at small sizes or for a few numbers or letters at larger sizes.

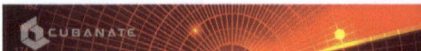

Unacceptable Executions

Stretched

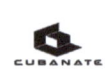

Compressed

Different colors

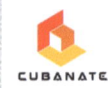

Non Core Colors

Illegible

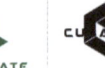

Outlined

Disordered

Alternately rotated

Blurred

Independently Rotated

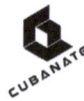

Exploded

Encircled

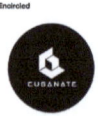

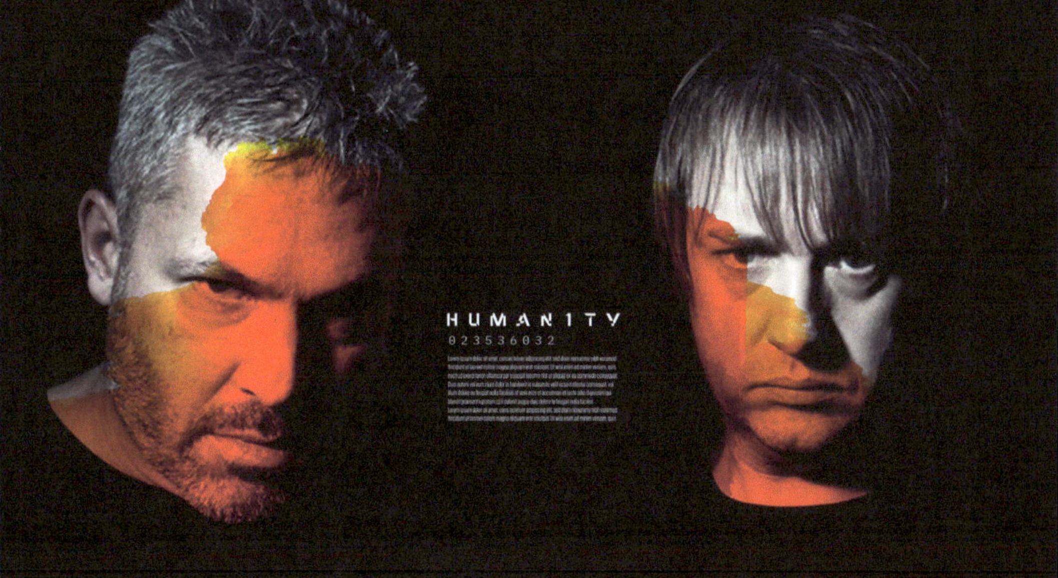

HUMAN1TY
023536032

Lorem ipsum dolor sit amet, consetetur sadipscing elitr, sed diam nonumy eirmod tempor invidunt ut labore et dolore magna aliquyam erat, sed diam voluptua. At vero eos et accusam et justo duo dolores et ea rebum. Stet clita kasd gubergren, no sea takimata sanctus est Lorem ipsum dolor sit amet. Lorem ipsum dolor sit amet, consetetur sadipscing elitr, sed diam nonumy eirmod tempor invidunt ut labore et dolore magna aliquyam erat, sed diam voluptua.

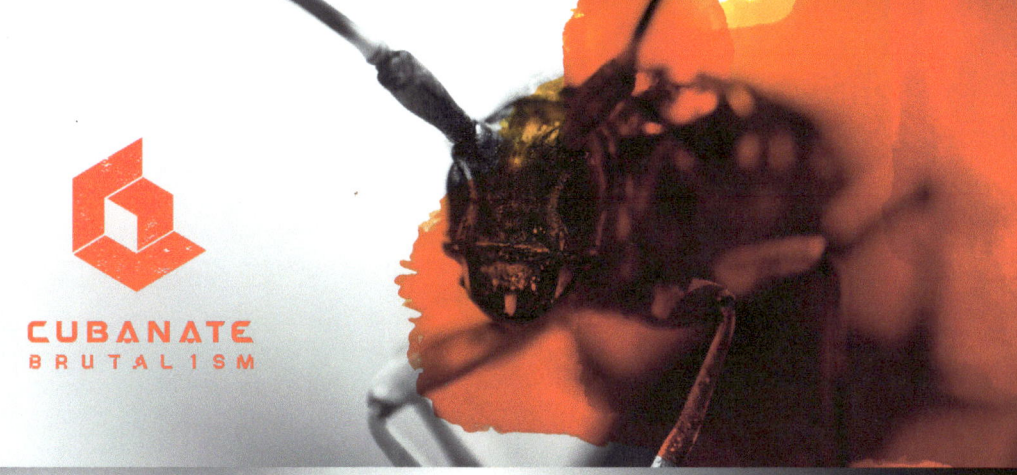

CUBANATE
BRUTAL1SM

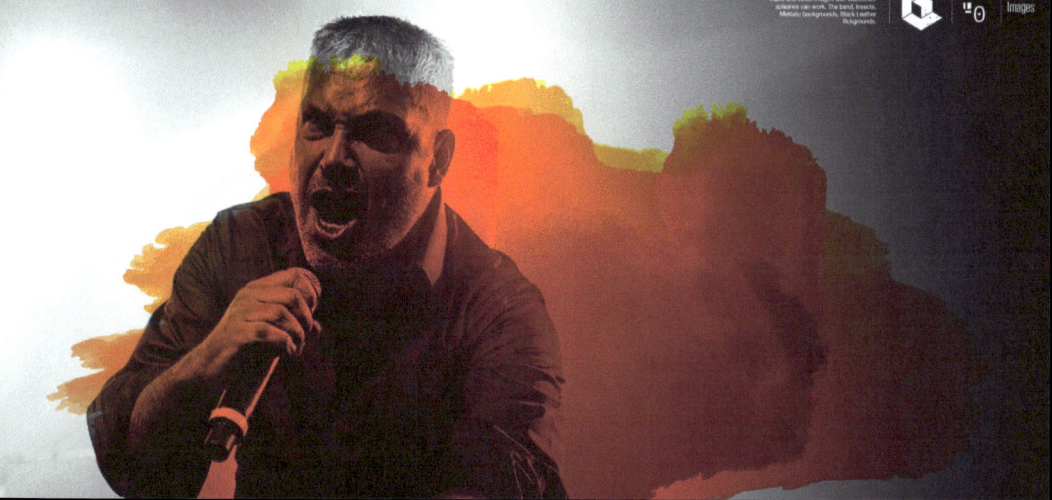

Black and White Images with Watercolor
splashes can work. The band. Insects.
Metallic backgrounds. Black Leather
Bckgrounds.

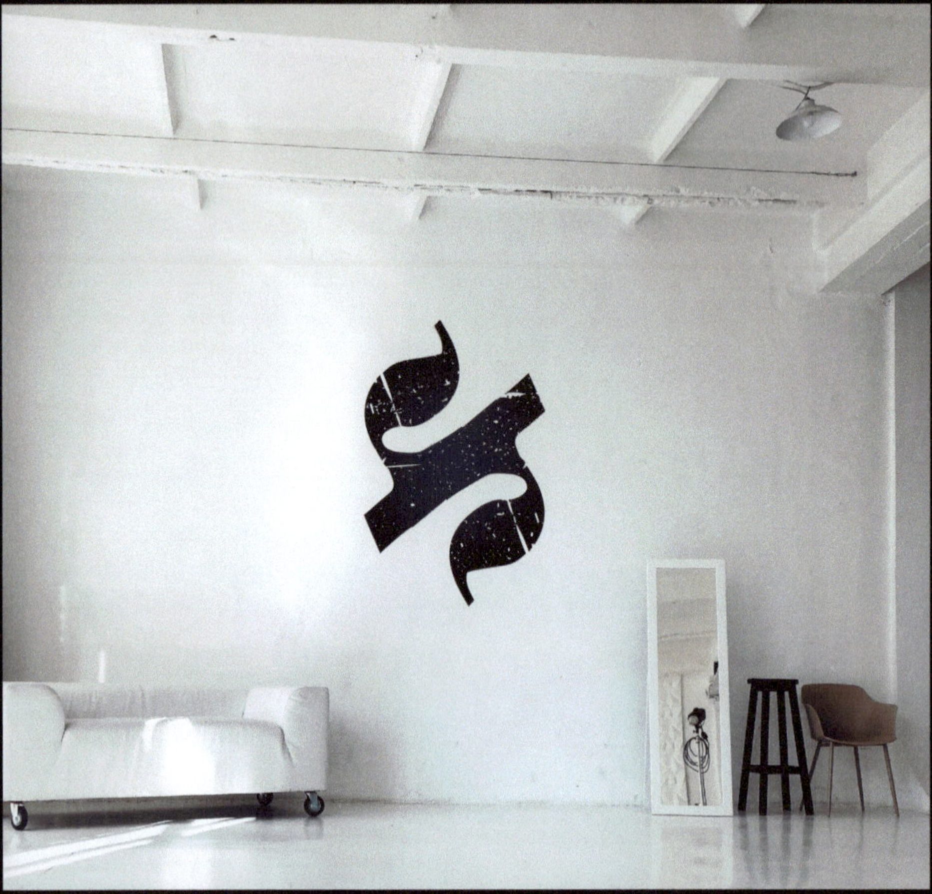

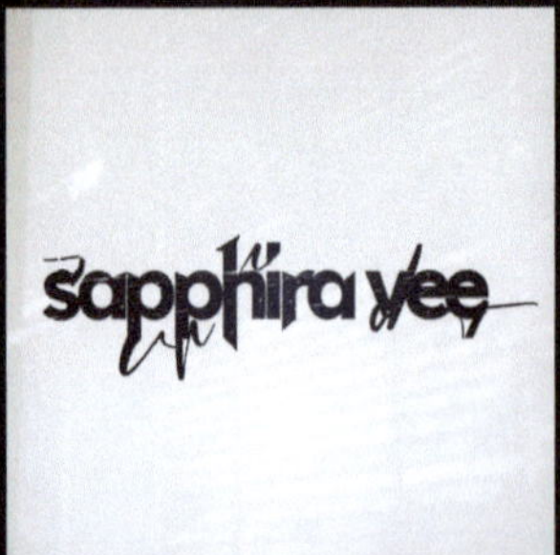

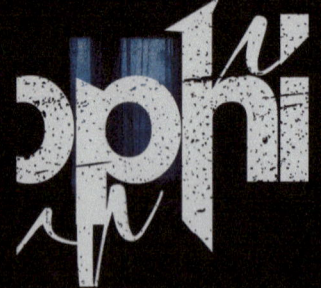

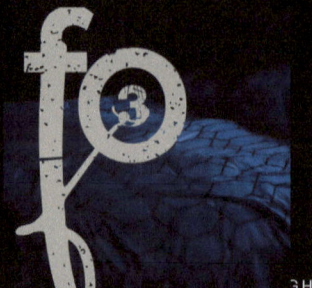
sapphira yee

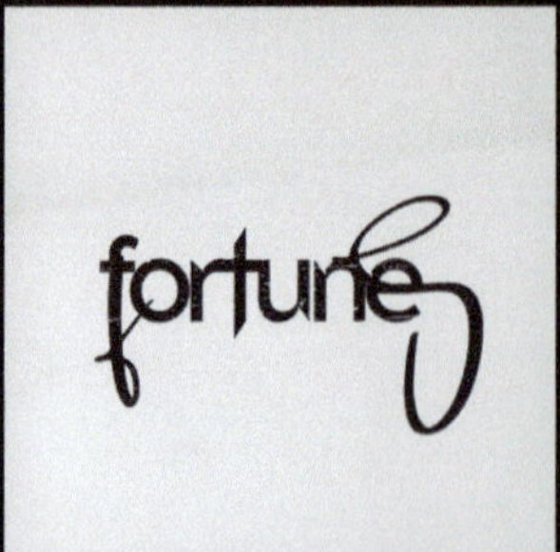

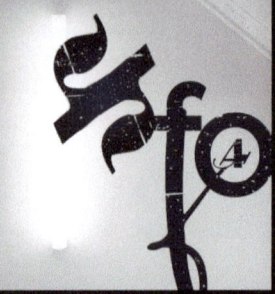

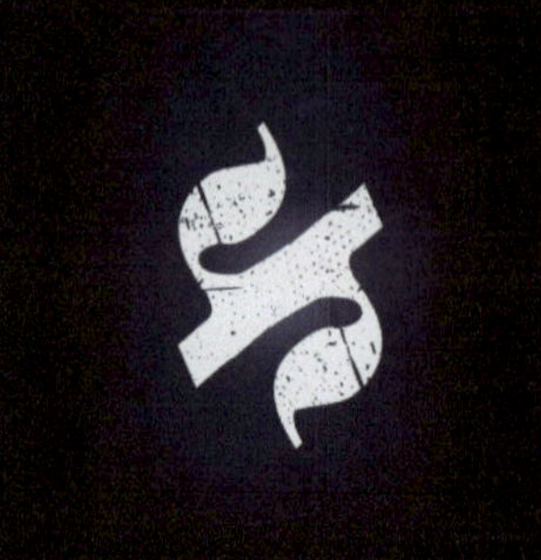

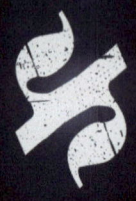

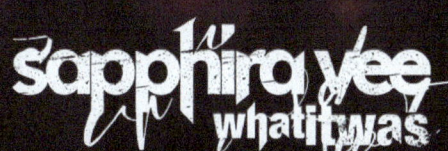

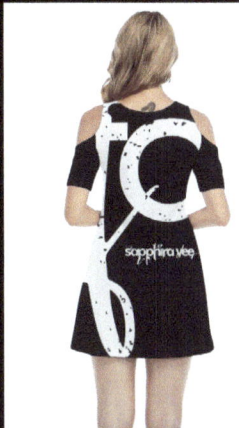
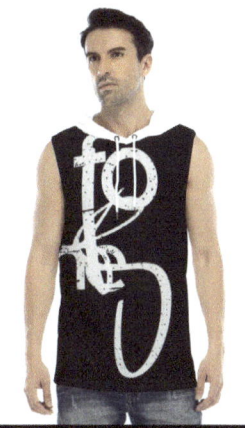
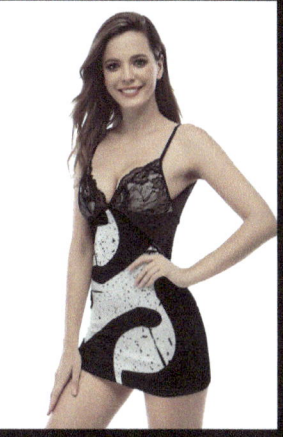

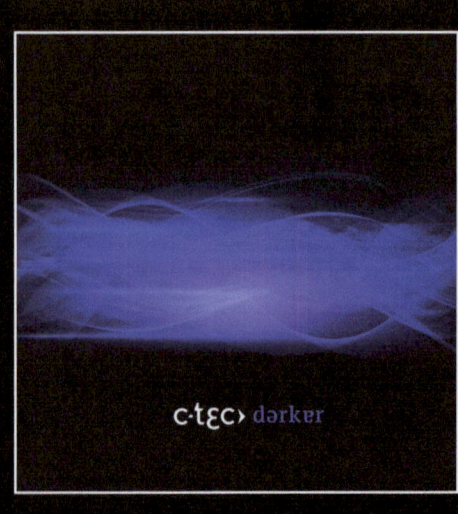

c·tɛc› dərkɛr

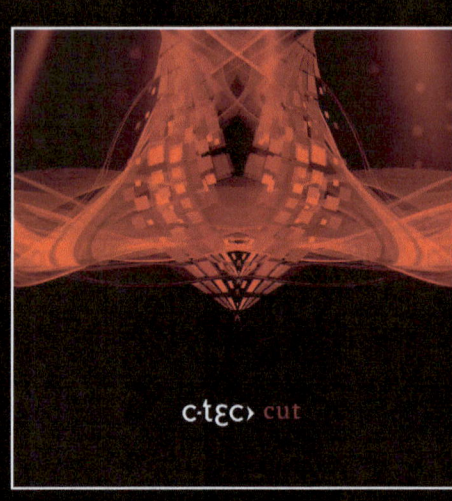

c·tɛc› cut

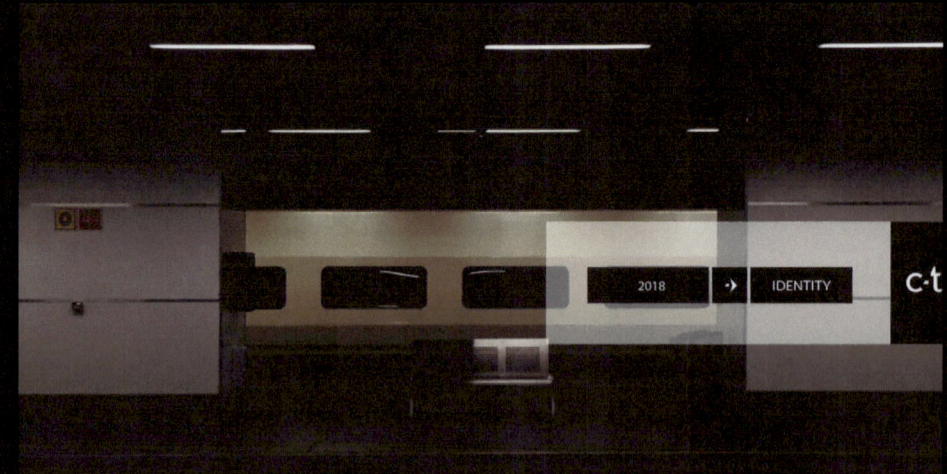

2018 ·› IDENTITY c·t

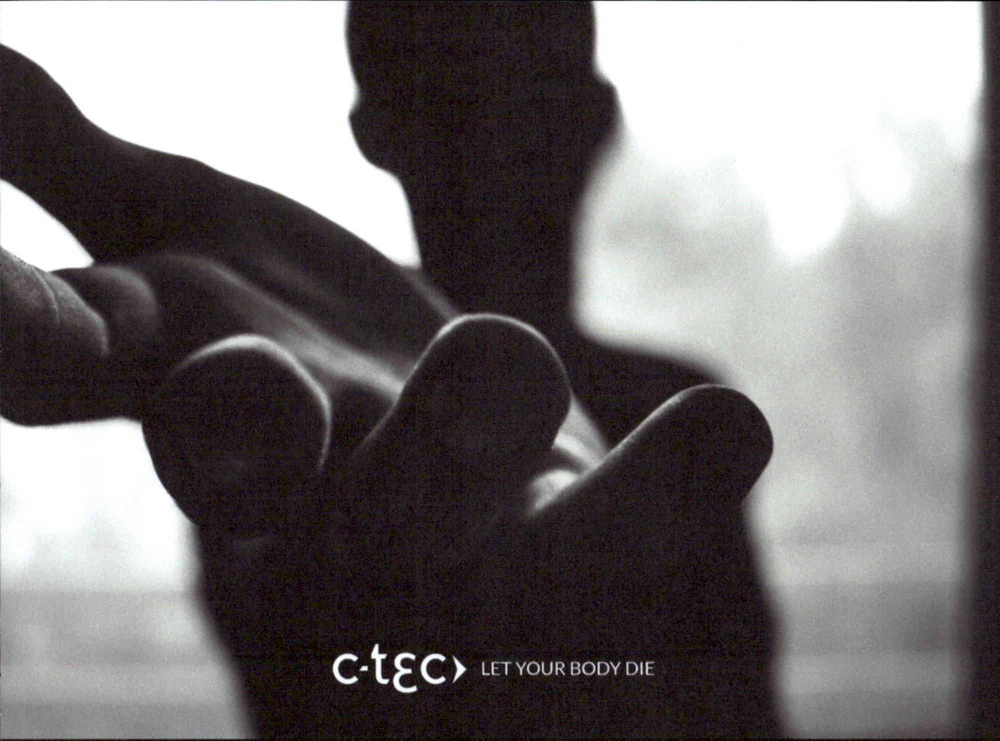

C·tƐC› LET YOUR BODY DIE

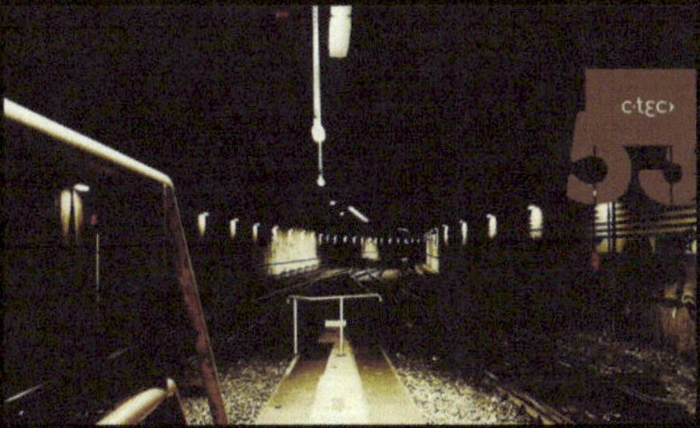

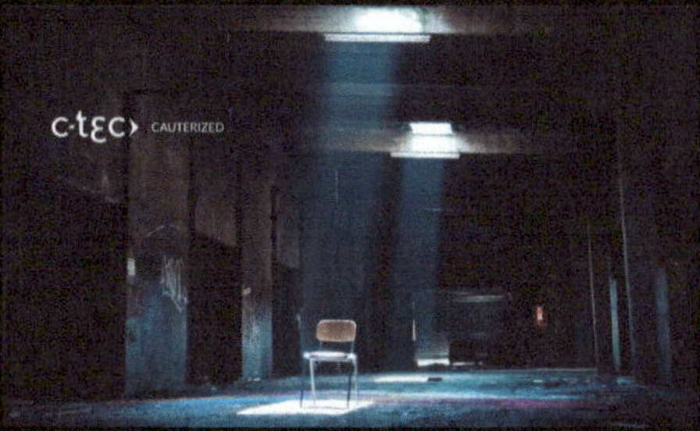

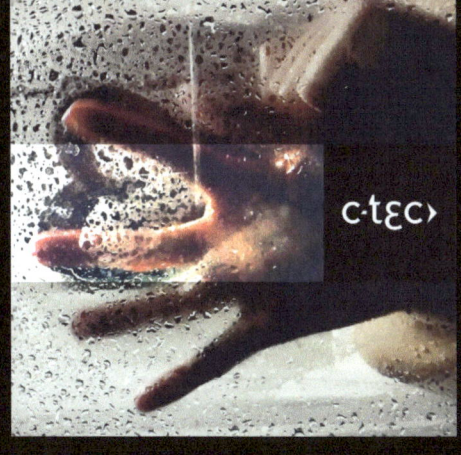

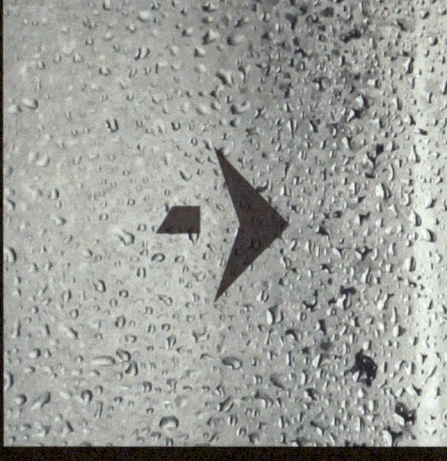

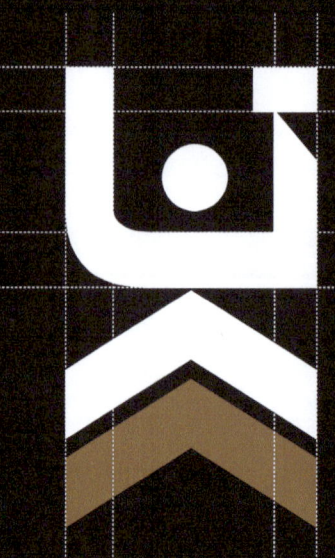

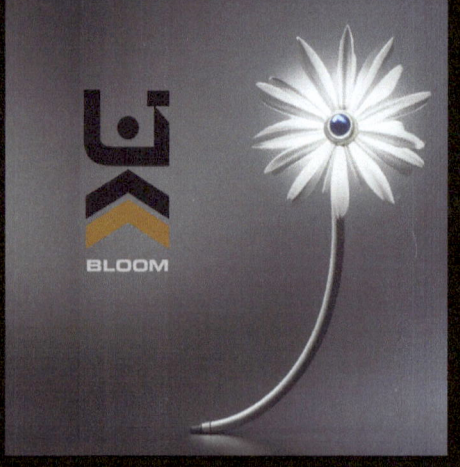

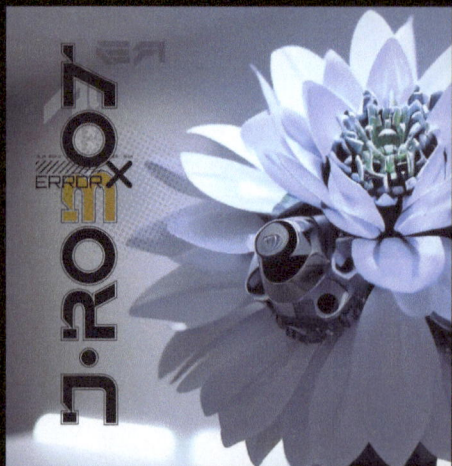

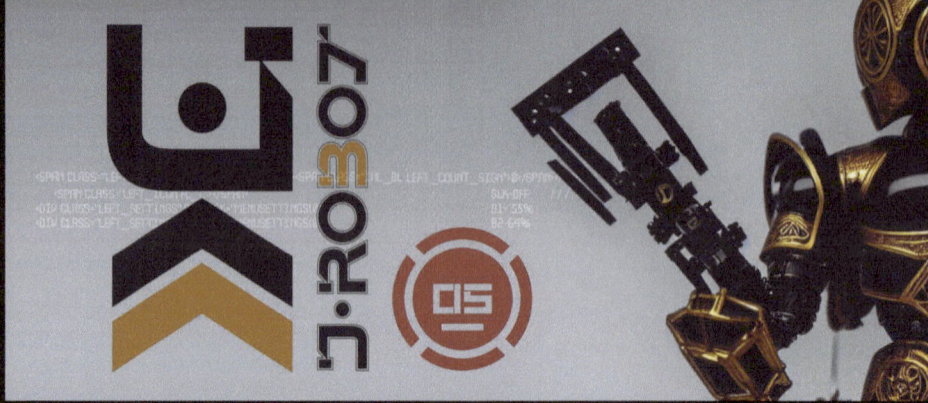

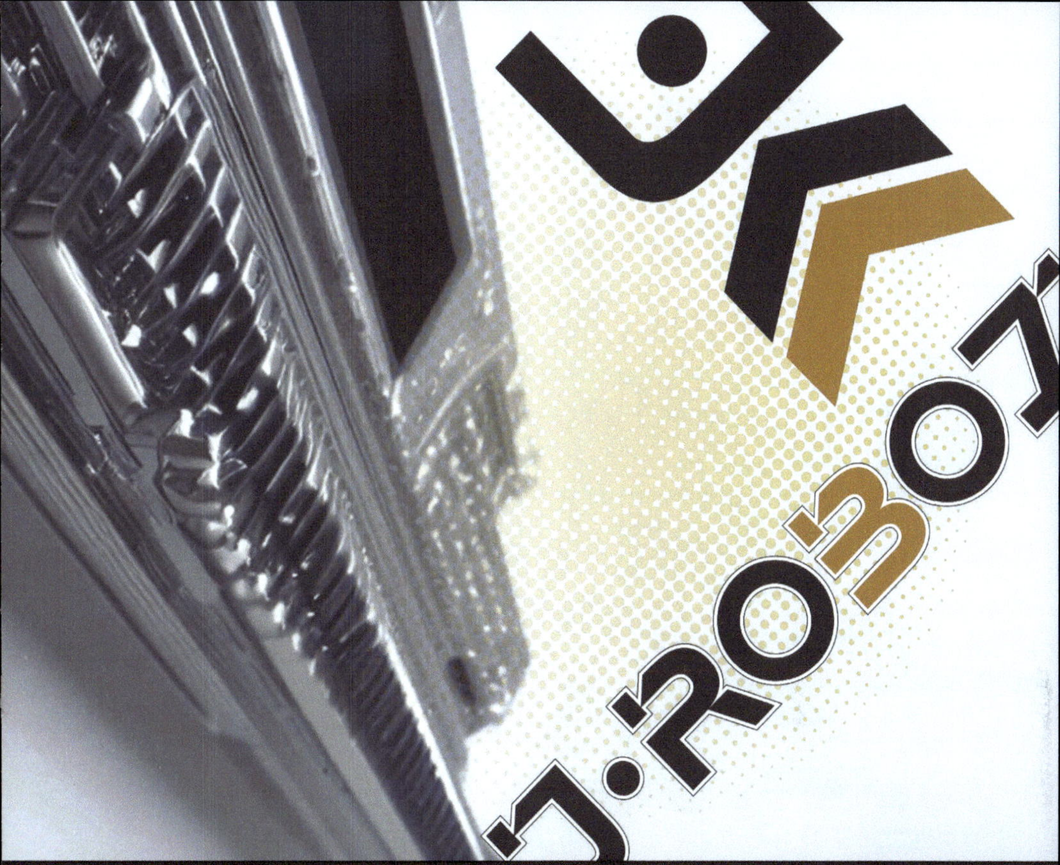

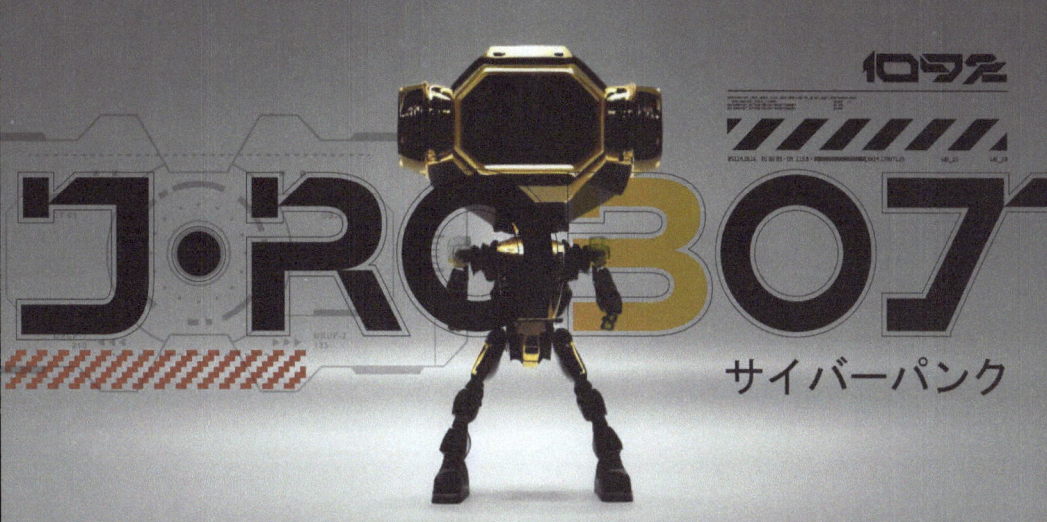

サイバーパンク

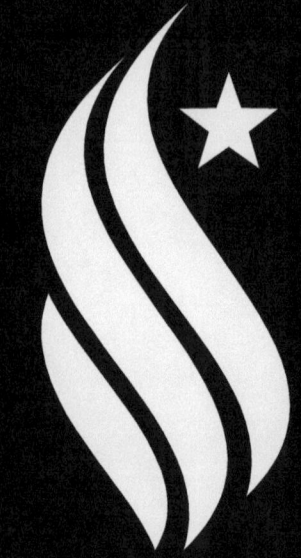

SUBSPACE

SUBSPACE

SUBAVERSARY 10 YEAR CELEBRATION EXTRAVAGANZA

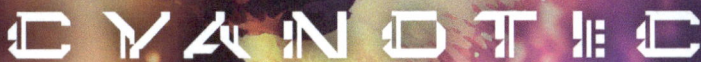

CHOKE CHAIN

CYANOTIC

LORELEI DREAMING

THE GOTHSICLES

Total Chroma

FEATURING

**CARRELLEE | NEVADA HARDWARE
THE OVERMORROW | DJ ECTO | DJ KITTENS**

| NOV | 25TH | 2023 | TICKETS ON SALE **FRIDAY, AUG 25TH** |

CRUCIBLE | MADISON WISCONSIN | 3116 COMMERCIAL AVE

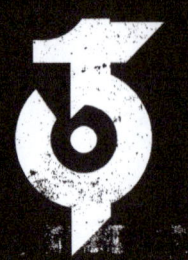

'IORQUE ORDER

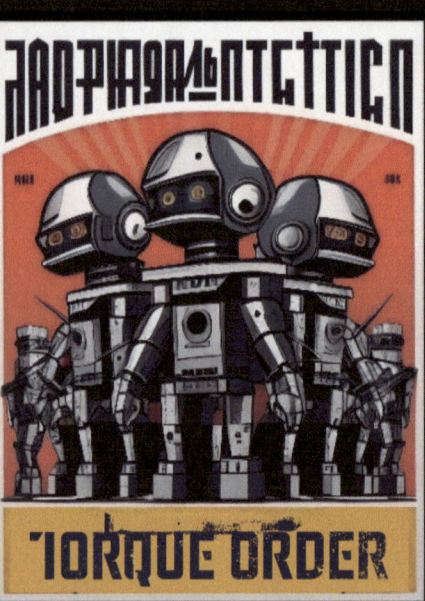

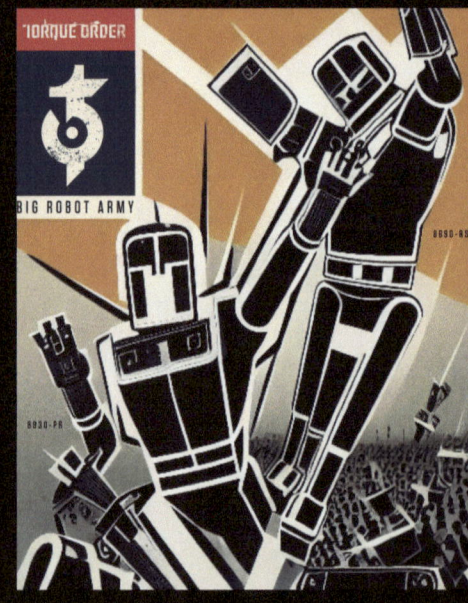

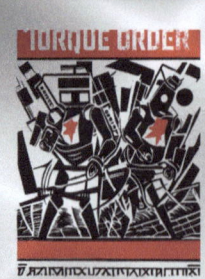

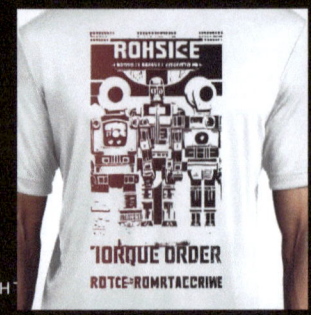

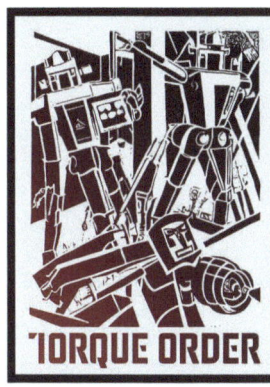
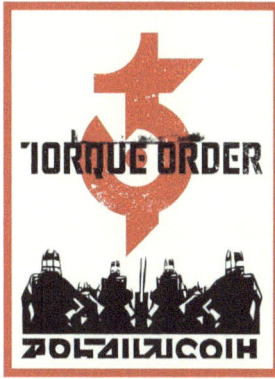
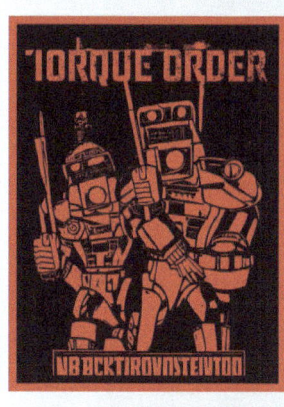
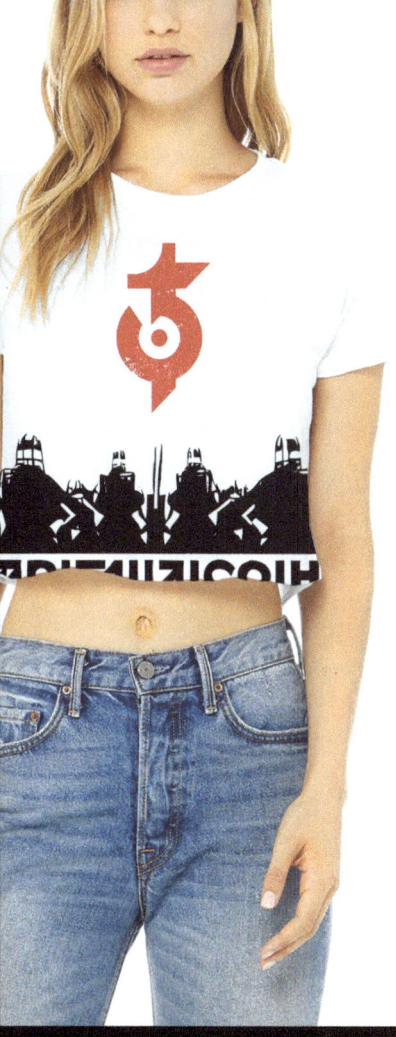
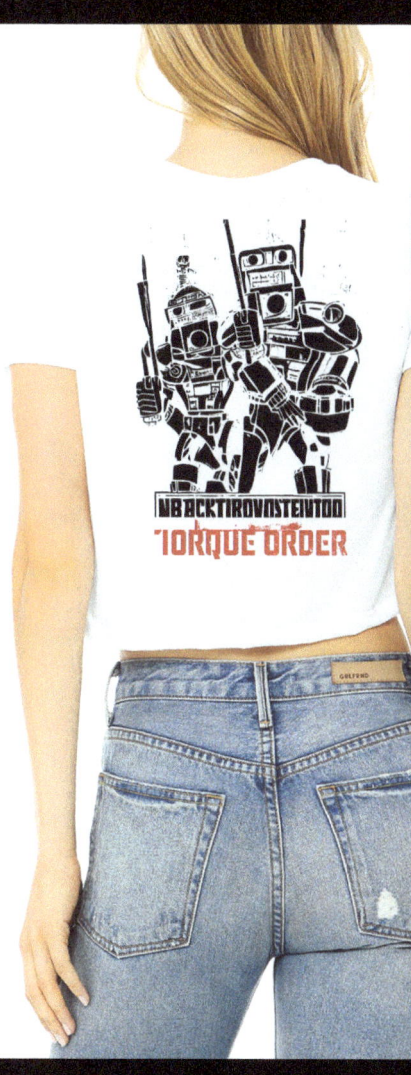

SILVER WALKS

songs of love and hate

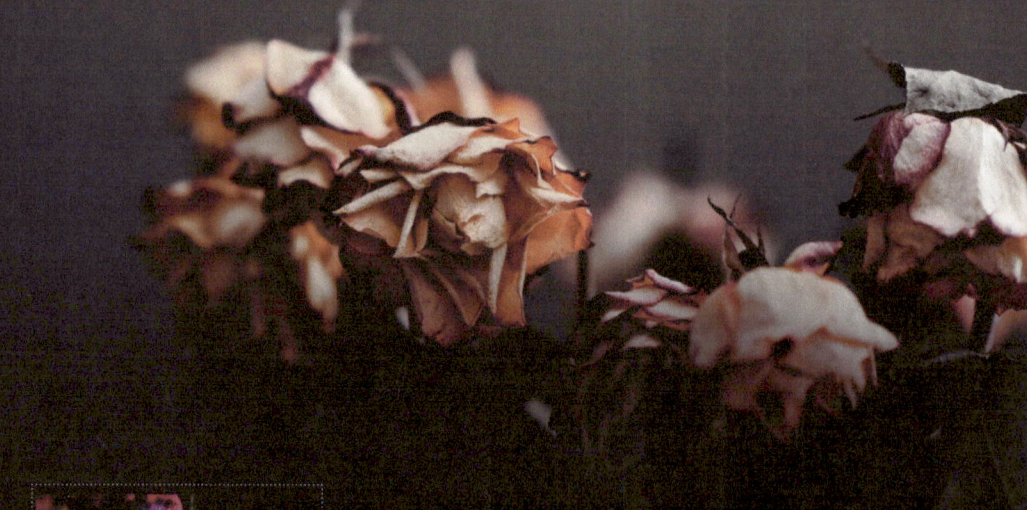

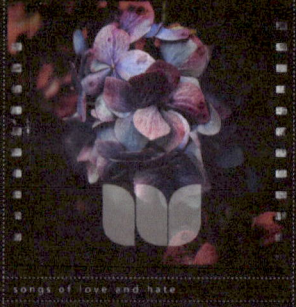

songs of love and hate

includes the single "tidal"
a distortion production
www.thesilverwalks.com | www.distortionprod.com

DST | PRO003 | **SW** | 2.0

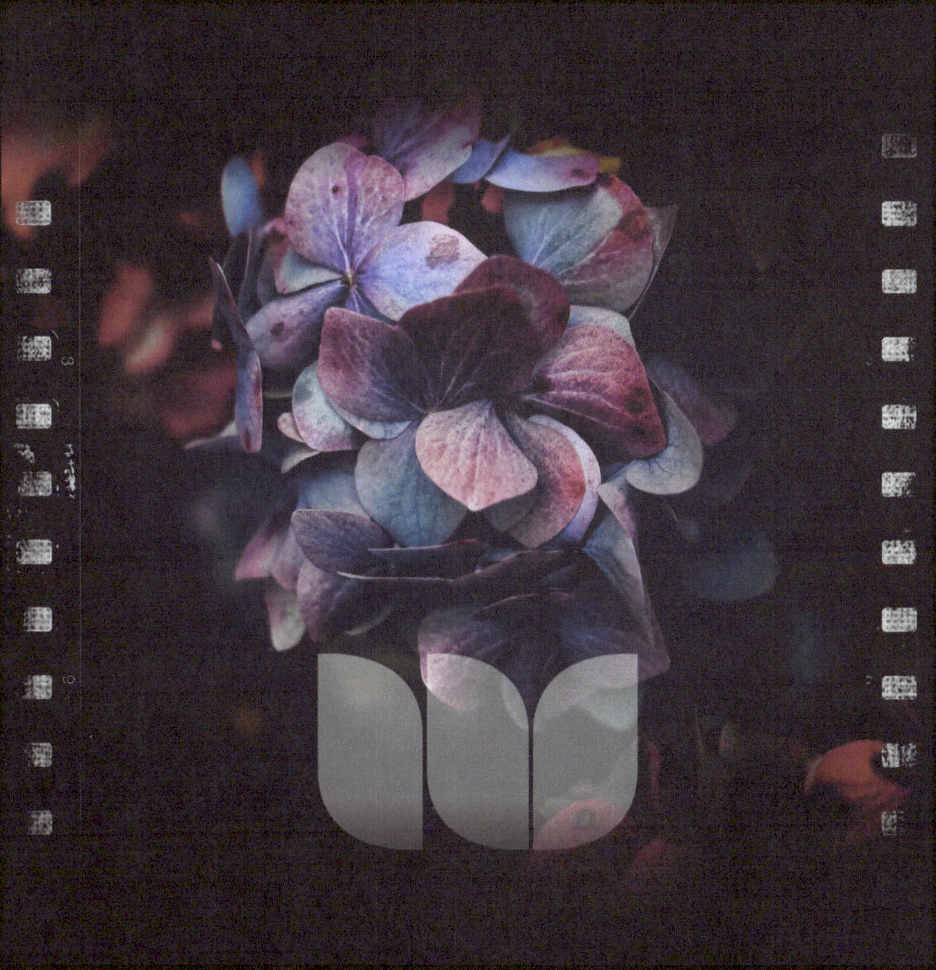

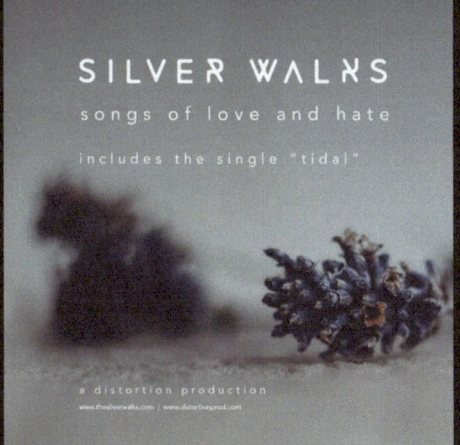

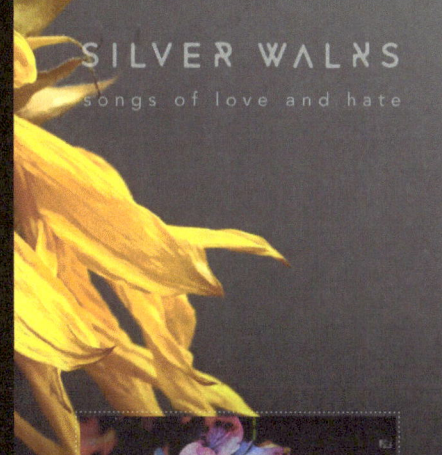

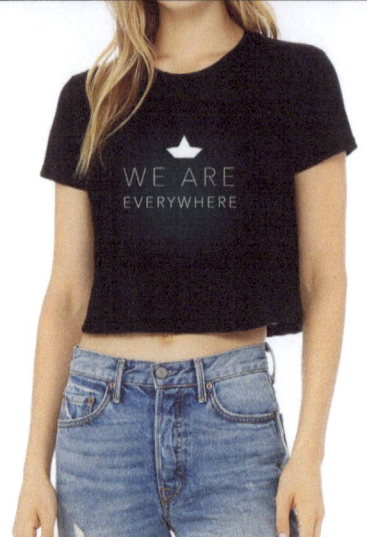
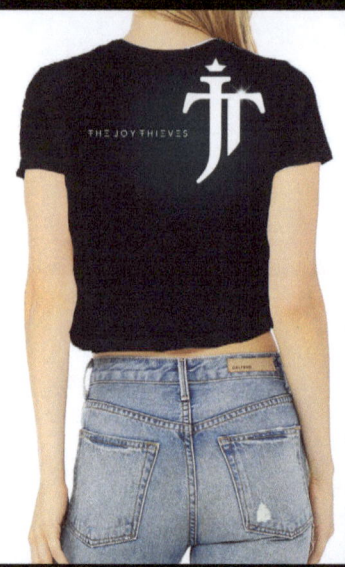

WE ARE
EVERYWHERE

THE JOY THIEVES

THE JOY THIEVES

UNEXPECTED HITS

VOL 1

NOT YOUR YOUR Property

MY MIND, MY Flesh IT BELONGS TO ME

FORCED BIRTH IS Murder

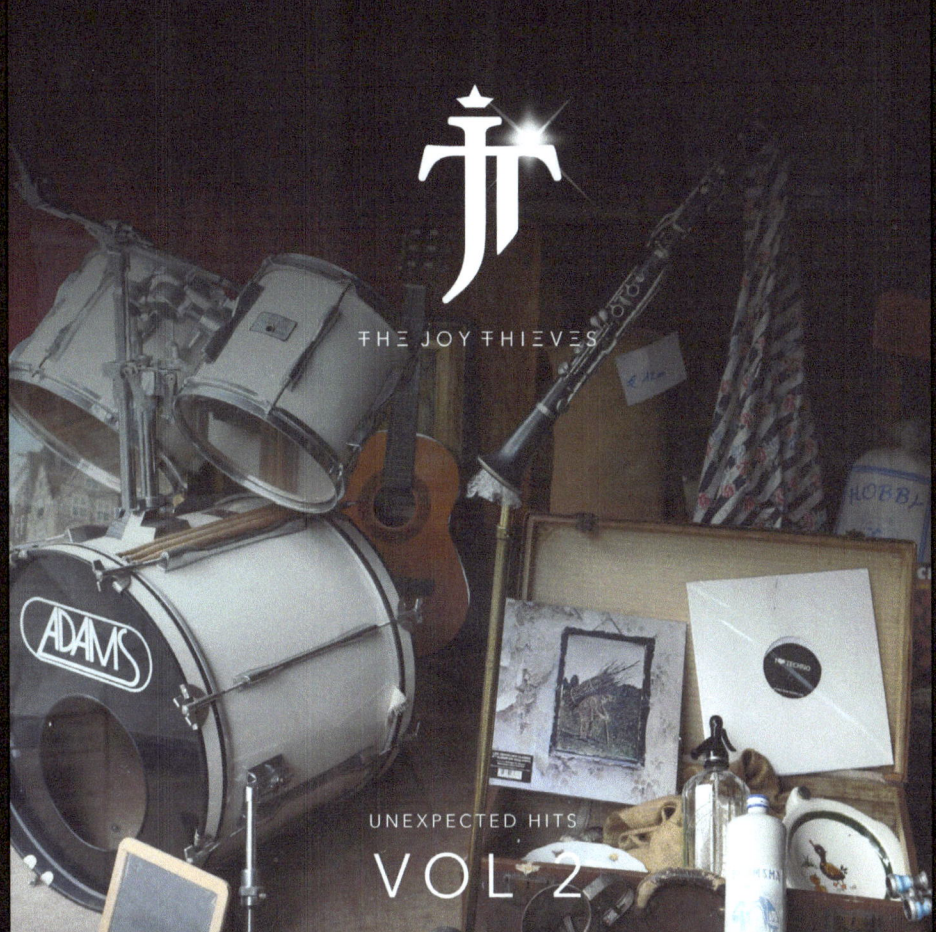

THE JOY THIEVES

UNEXPECTED HITS

VOL 2

retcon

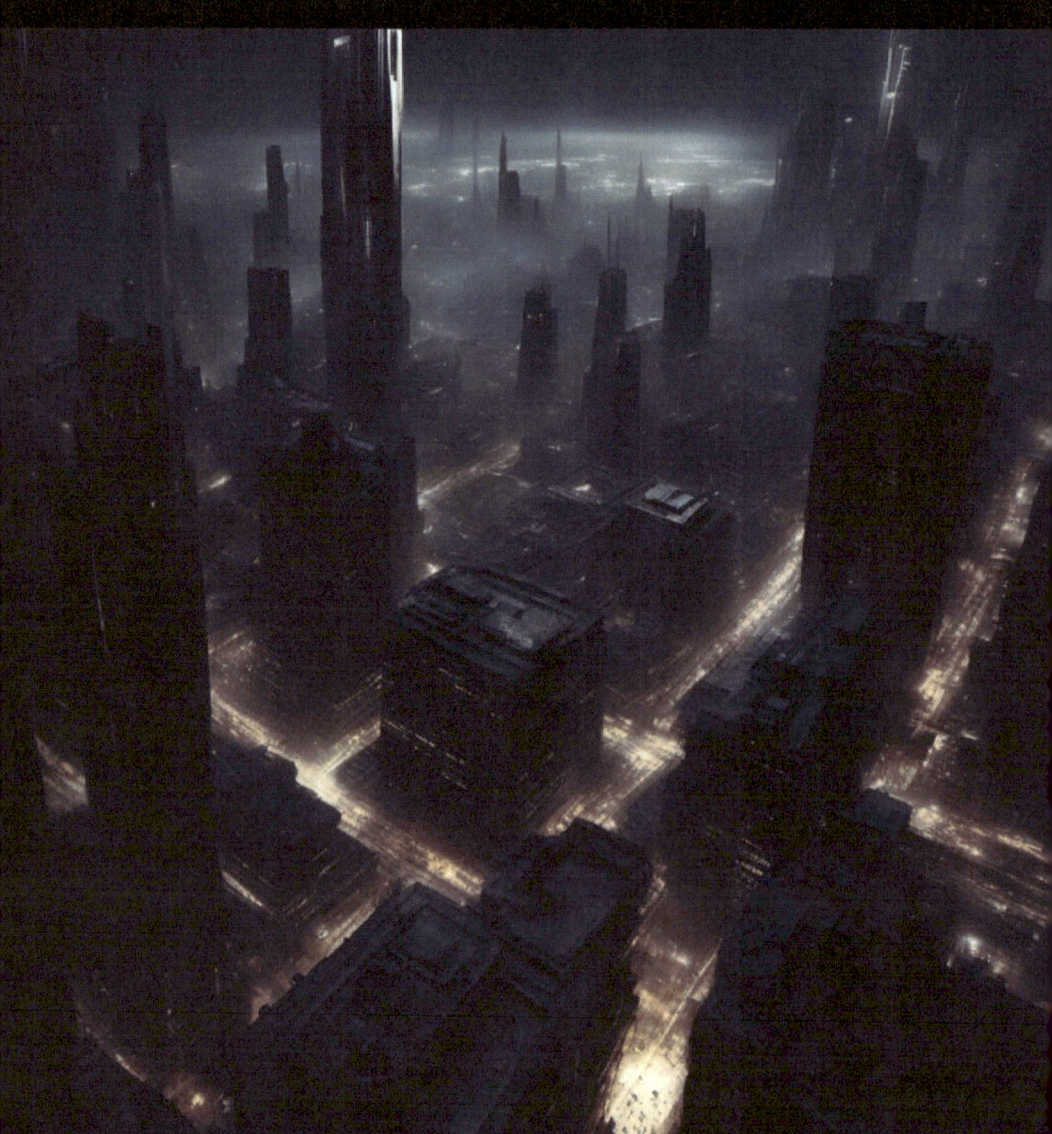

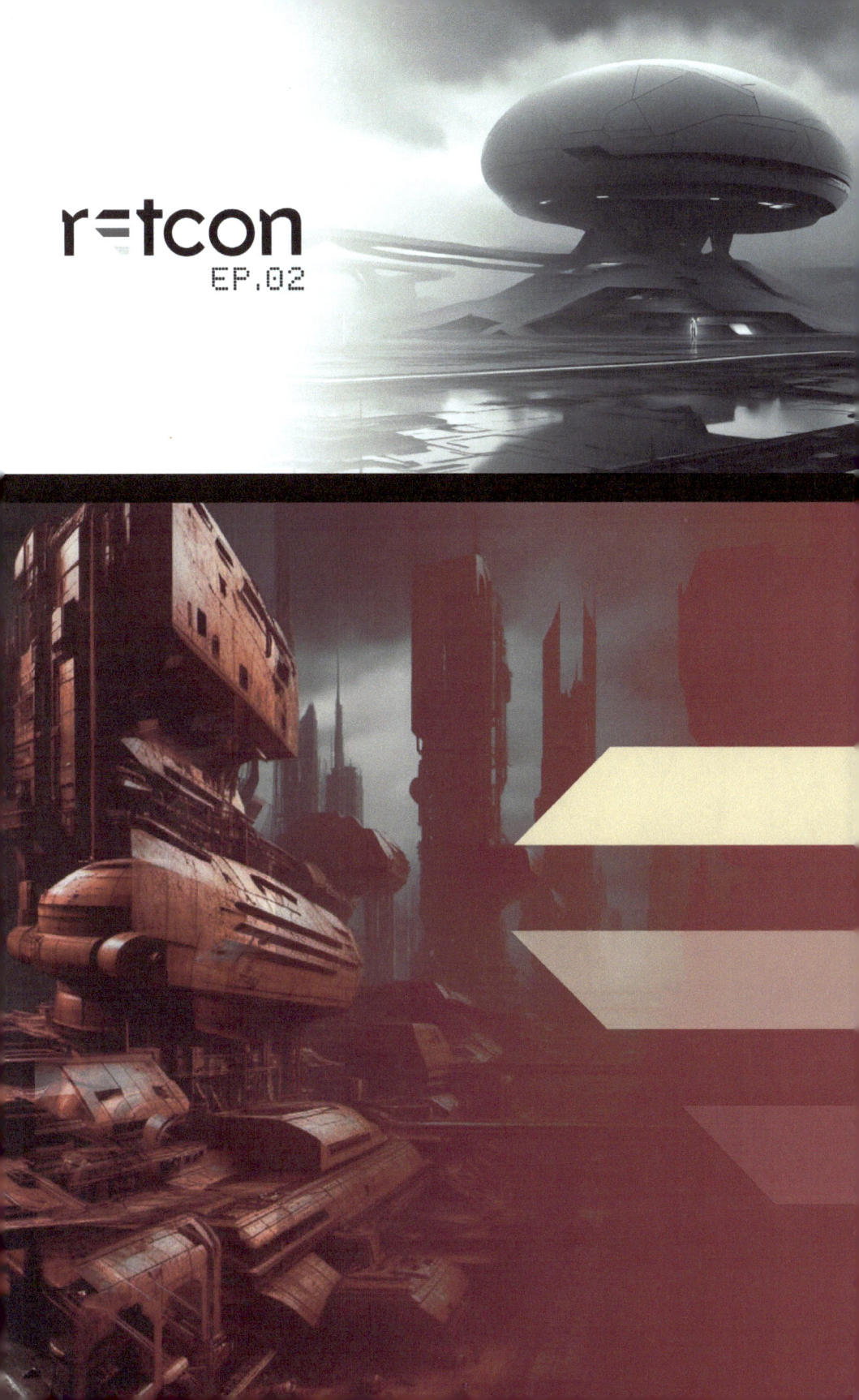

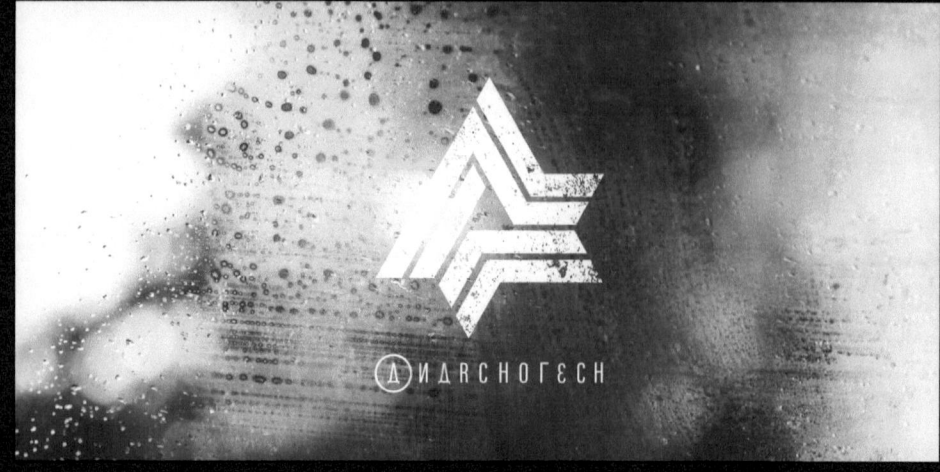

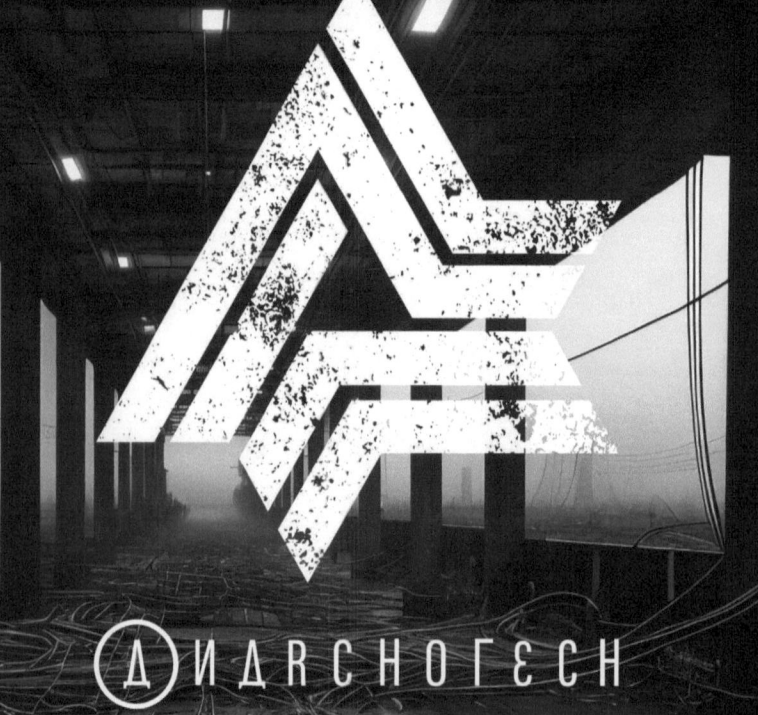

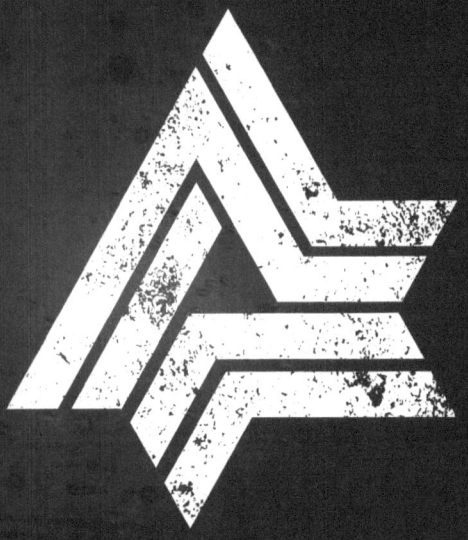

ΛИΛRCHOΓECH

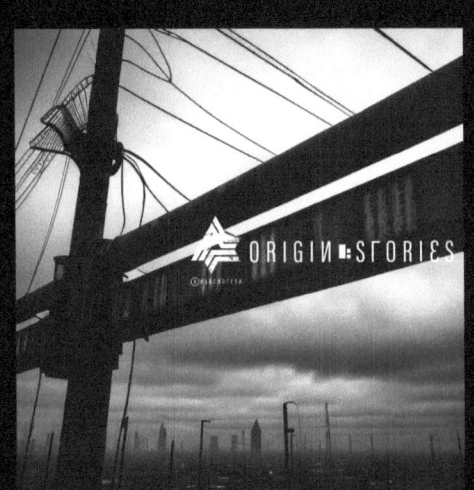

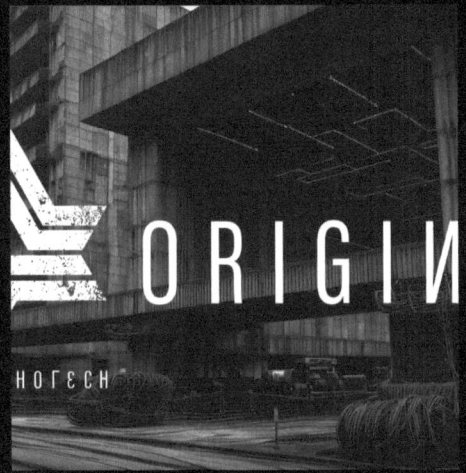

A COVENANT OF THORNS

ACOT

Λ COVENANT OF ᚦHORNS

Segoe UI

Titling and Body Copy

Regular
ABCDEFGHIJKLMNOPQRSTUVWXYZ
abcdefghijklmnopqrstuvwxyz0123456789
ÄÀÂÃÅÆÇDÉÈÊÉÍÏÍÑÓÒÔÕØ

Bold
ABCDEFGHIJKLMNOPQRSTUVWXYZ
abcdefghijklmnopqrstuvwxyz0123456789
ÄÀÂÃÅÆÇDÉÈÊÉÍÏÍÑÓÒÔÕØ

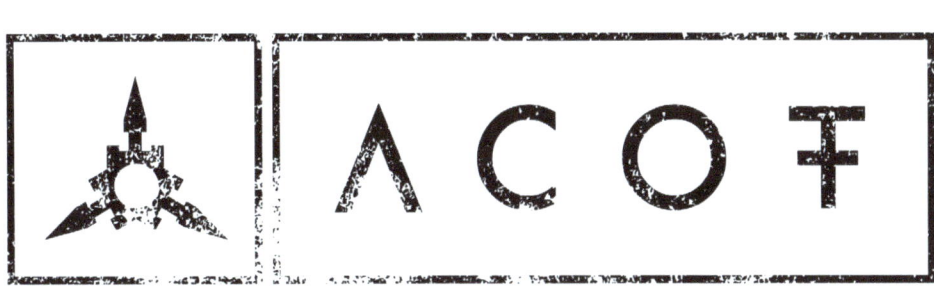

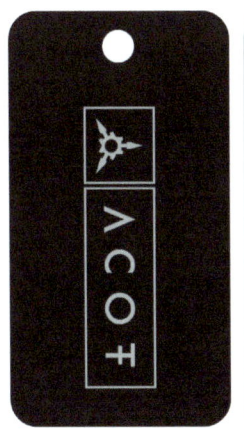

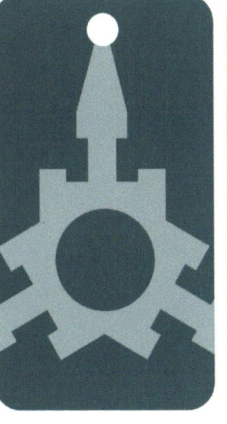

A COVENANT OF ᚦHORNS

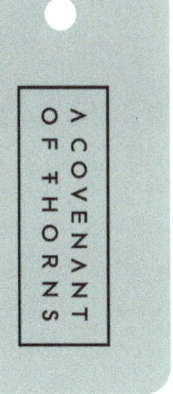

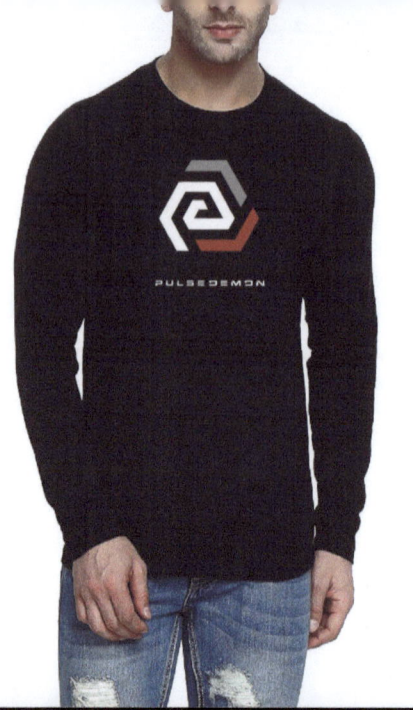

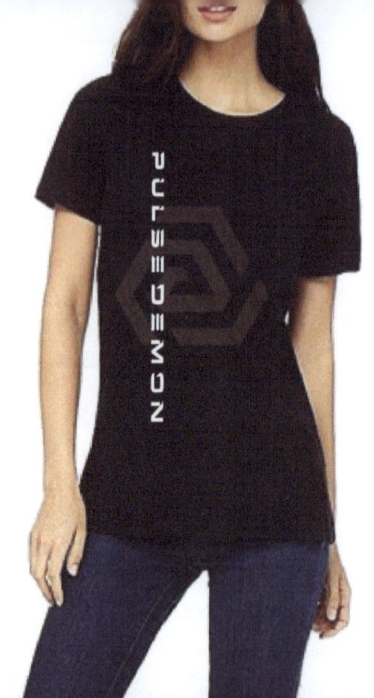

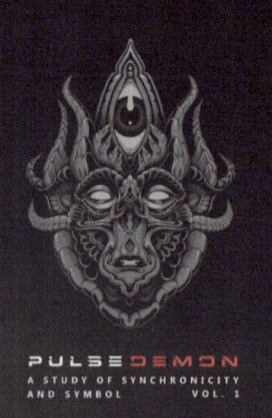

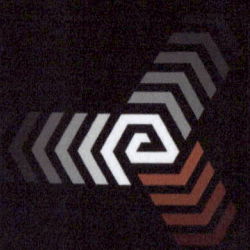

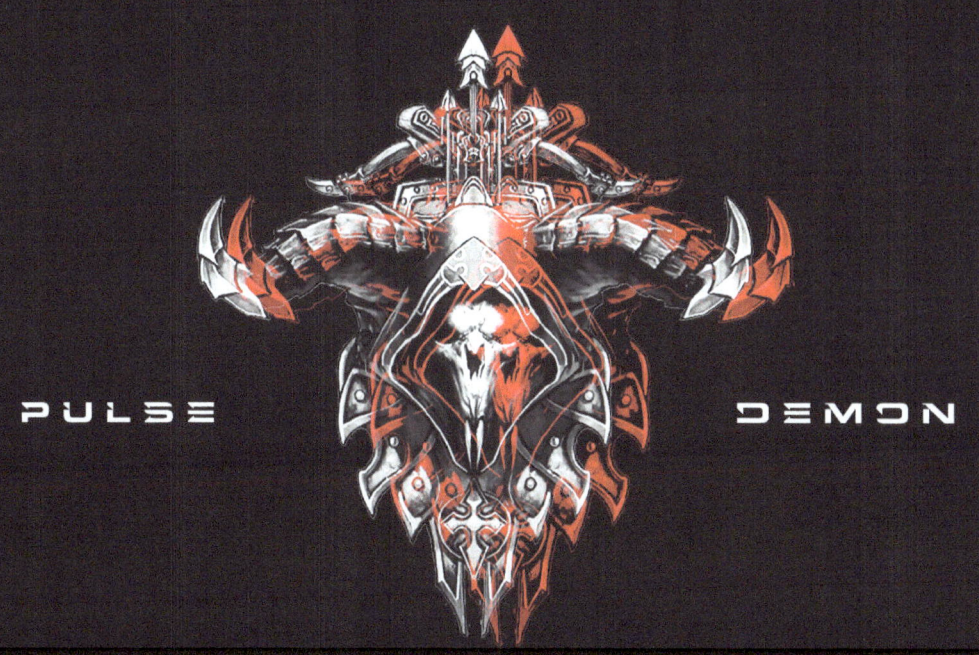

PULSE DEMON

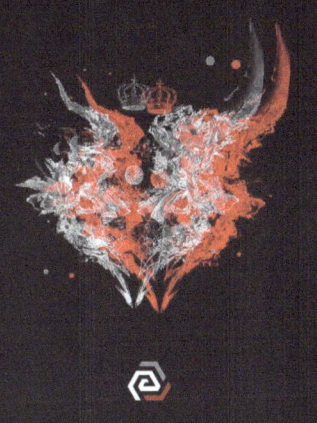

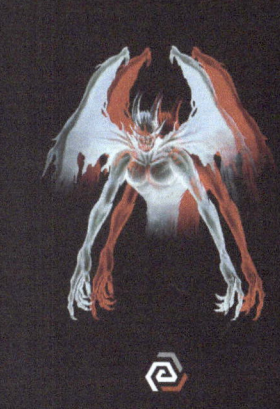

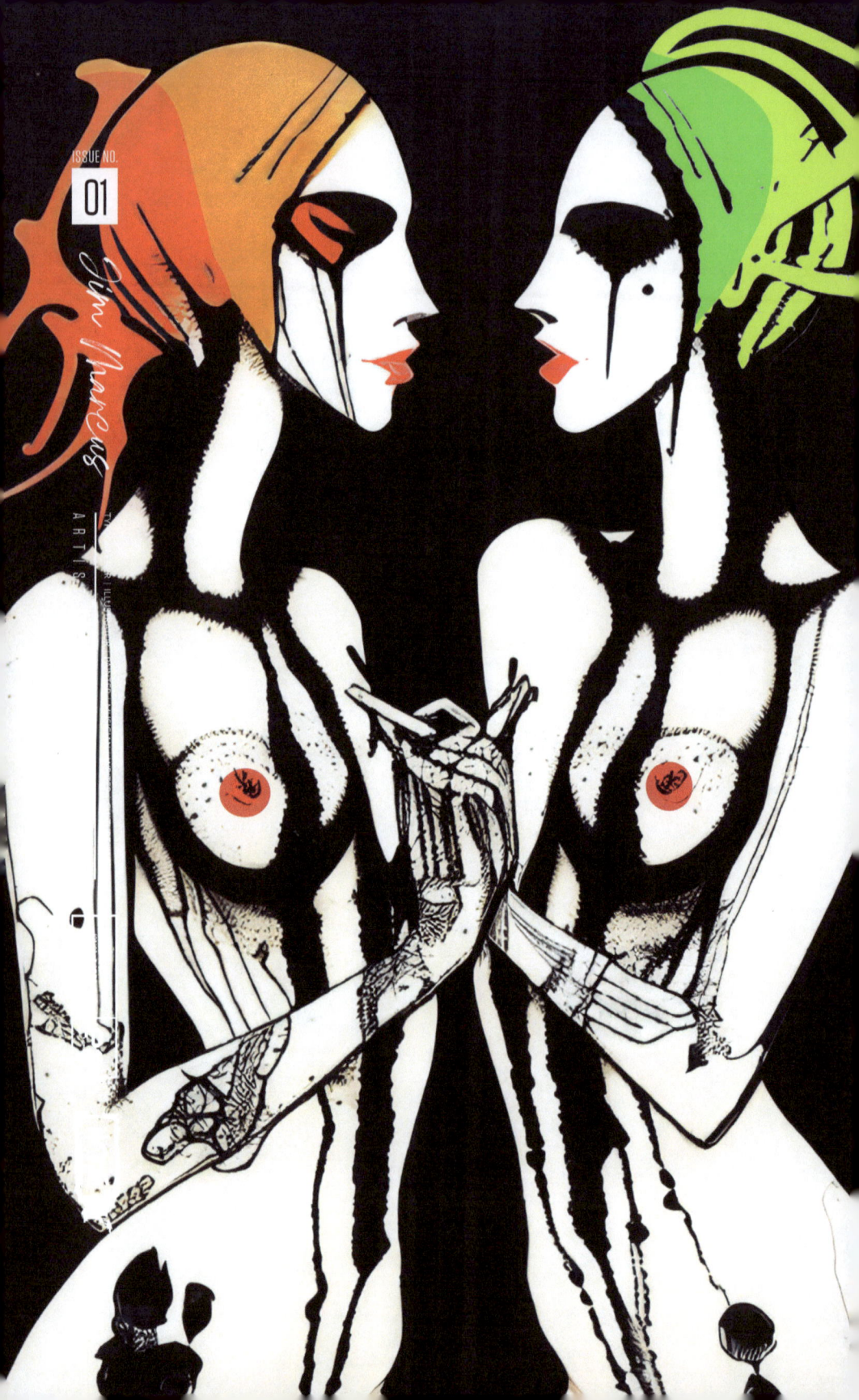

www.ingramcontent.com/pod-product-compliance
Lightning Source LLC
Chambersburg PA
CBHW040319010626
45792CB00024B/2069